PUE

Grande

PUEBLOS

of the Rio Grande

A Visitor's Guide

DANIEL
GIBSON

RIO NUEVO PUBLISHERS
TUCSON, ARIZONA

This book is dedicated to my
brothers and sisters—David Gibson,
Brett Solon, Gretchen Schaffer, and
Matt Gibson—who have always
encouraged and supported me in my
work and life.

cover: *Traditional dancer, Zuni;
kiva wall, San Ildefonso*
STEPHEN TRIMBLE

back cover: *Deer dancer figurine
by Louis Naranjo, Cochiti*
MARK NOHL

half title page: *Kossa clowns,
San Juan, 1935*
T. HARMON PARKHURST

title page: *Laguna, 1883*
BEN WITTICK

table of contents: *On the
Rio Grande, Isleta, 1905*
EDWARD S. CURTIS

Rio Nuevo Publishers ®
P.O. Box 5250
Tucson, AZ 85703-0250
520-623-9558
www.rionuevo.com

Text © 2001 Daniel Gibson
All Rights Reserved
Photographs © Deb Friedrichs,
Mark Nohl, and Stephen Trimble
as credited.
All archival photographs courtesy
Museum of New Mexico.
(Details page 106.)

Editor: Ronald J. Foreman
Design: Larry Lindahl,
    Lindahl-Bryant Studio, Sedona
Map: Deborah Reade and Kevin Kibsey

Printed in Korea

10 9 8 7 6 5 4 3 2

Library of Congress Cataloging-in-Publication Data
Gibson, Daniel.
        Pueblos of the Rio Grande: a visitor's guide / Daniel Gibson.
            p. cm.
        ISBN: 1-887896-26-0
1. Pueblos—New Mexico—Guidebooks. 2. Pueblo Indians—New Mexico.
3. New Mexico—Guidebooks. I. Title.
        E99.P9 G52 2001
        917.89'0454—dc21   2001004625

CONTENTS

Pueblos of the Rio Grande

UTAH

SAN JUAN MOUNTAINS

Rio Grande

Blanca Peak

Hovenweep National Monument Headquarters

LA PLATA MOUNTAINS

Mesa Verde Nat. Park

Hesperus Peak

666

Cortez

Durango

Sleeping Ute Mt.

UTE MT. UTE

Mancos R.

Aztec Ruins Nat. Mon.

SOUTHERN UTE

COLORADO
NEW MEXICO

Continental Divide

Blue Hill

Blue Hill

San Juan

Farmington

Navajo Lake

Dulce

Blue Lake

La Plata River

Animas River

Shiprock

Ship Rock

Salmon Ruins

Canyon Largo

JICARILLA APACHE

TAOS

68

Table Mesa

Barber Peak

Angel Peak

Gobernador Can.

Taos

CHUSKA MOUNTAINS

Carson's

550

Huerfano Mountain

SAN ILDEFONSO

PICURIS

76

Bisti Badlands

Nageezi

SANTA CLARA

SAN JUAN

666

N A V A J O

Counselors

Bandelier Nat. Mon.

NAMBE

Sheep Spgs.

Lake Valley

Cuba

JEMEZ MTS.

TESUQUE

POJOAQUE

SANGRE DE CRISTO MOUNTAINS

Chaco Culture Nat. Historical Park

550

4

84 285

Santa Fe

Tohatchi

Torreon

JEMEZ

Pecos River

Crownpoint

ZIA

COCHITI

25

Window Rock

Red Rock State Park

Casamero Ruins

ZIA

SANTO DOMINGO

Pecos Nat. Historical Park

Gallup

Ft. Wingate

TÓ HAJIILEE NAVAJO

Rio Puerco

SANTA ANA

SAN FELIPE

40

61

Old Fort Wingate

Mt. Taylor

LAGUNA

Petroglyph Nat. Mon.

Coronado State Mon.

SANDIA

SANDIA MTS.

Rio San José

Zuni R.

Grants

Rio

San José

Albuquerque

40

Corn Mt.

ZUNI MTS.

ZUNI

LAGUNA

ISLETA

MANZANO MTS.

RAMAH NAVAJO

El Morro National Monument

ACOMA

El Malpais Nat. Mon.

Continental Divide

LAGUNA

ALAMO NAVAJO

(of the East)

Rio Grande

■ (Quarai)

N

(Abo) ■

Salinas Pueblo Missions National Monument

ARIZONA

0   20   40

MILES

■ (Gran Quivira)

Socorro

25

INTRODUCTION

Laguna vendors meet the train, 1883
WILLIAM HENRY JACKSON

WHEN I WAS A BOY growing up in the 1960s, I took a summer train trip from Colorado to my hometown of Albuquerque, New Mexico. I awoke as the train was descending from the grassy mesa flanking the Rio Grande, and as I looked out the window I saw a remarkable scene. There alongside the river, basking in the warmth of the morning sun, stood the picturesque adobe pueblo village of San Felipe. Dozens of suntanned children were racing along the riverbank and splashing in the shallows. Women who had come to the river to wash clothes looked up and waved as the silvery rail cars of our train clacked by. I remember waving back until the pueblo receded from view.

The same scene does not greet train passengers as they pass by San Felipe Pueblo today.

No one washes clothes in the river anymore (those residents who don't own a washing machine now take their loads to a Laundromat), and kids seldom play in the river. But in most respects, a visitor will find life at San Felipe or any of the other nineteen pueblos of New Mexico to be remarkably unchanged.

In a nation that prides itself on constant change, where so many native peoples have been displaced or overwhelmed by the relentless expansion of the dominant culture, the Pueblo people have managed to hold fast to the lands and traditions that have sustained them since time immemorial. They have done so despite centuries of oppression, armed conflict, massive epidemics, and social, political, and economic isolation, which is a testament to their character and determination.

The Pueblo peoples today remain true to their cultural and spiritual roots. Like their ancestors, they believe in making uncommon sacrifices for the common good, and in striving, collectively and in all things, to achieve harmony with the natural world.

Pueblo History

PREHISTORY

About eleven thousand years ago, while much of North America lay under the glaciers of the last Ice Age, Paleolithic hunter-gatherers migrated to what is now the American Southwest. Here, the ice and snow pack was limited to the high mountains, and game was abundant in the more temperate valleys below.

Around 2000 B.C., people living in the Southwest learned how to farm from Mexican Indian cultures to the south. By 500 B.C., once-nomadic groups living in the San Juan River drainage had established semi-permanent villages near their cultivated fields of corn, beans, and squash. They also had learned to weave elaborate baskets with which to carry and store the harvest.

These Basketmakers initially lived in subterranean pithouses of earth and wood, but sometime between the sixth and eighth centuries A.D. the more progressive among them began to build aboveground, masonry homes, expand their trade networks, and refine their arts and religious rituals.

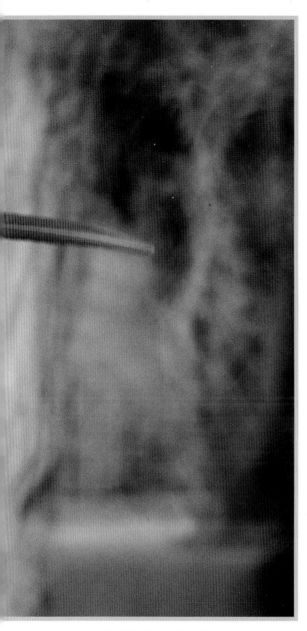

Buffalo dancer, San Ildefonso
STEPHEN TRIMBLE

Archeologists call these innovators the Pueblo I culture, but they also came to be popularly known as the Anasazi, which is a Navajo word meaning "ancient enemies" or "enemy ancestors." Contemporary Pueblo peoples have long objected to the use of this term, and have made a convincing argument that "Ancestral Pueblo" is more accurate and respectful.

Between A.D. 900 and 1170, the Ancestral Pueblo culture achieved a cultural high-water mark of sorts at Chaco Canyon in what is now northwestern New Mexico. There the people built dozens of great houses, including Pueblo Bonito, which rose four or five stories high and contained more than six hundred fifty rooms.

The archeological record suggests that Chaco was something of a ceremonial and trading center of the Ancestral Pueblo world. From Chaco Canyon itself, a network of 30-foot-wide roadways leads to many of the more than one hundred outlying great houses located throughout the Colorado Plateau. The roads are especially intriguing because the Ancestral Pueblo people had neither wheeled vehicles nor beasts of burden.

During roughly the same period, in what is now southwestern Colorado, other Ancestral Pueblo people were building great houses in the Montezuma Valley and large-scale cliff dwellings in the rugged canyons of Mesa Verde, at the base of the San Juan Mountains.

The archeological record confirms that Ancestral Pueblo people began leaving Chaco Canyon in the twelfth century for points east, west, and south. In the late thirteenth century they began to abandon the Mesa Verde area, as well. By A.D. 1300, the San Juan River drainage was largely deserted. The exodus may have been precipitated by a devastating twenty-year drought that began in A.D. 1276. Also, the demands of a burgeoning population may have outstripped available resources, which may in turn have led to internal conflicts and warfare.

Whatever the case, Pueblo peoples ultimately found refuge in the valleys of the Rio Grande and its tributaries, as well as the Zuni River drainage and the Hopi mesas of northeastern Arizona. Over time, the various pueblos they established emerged as culturally distinct and autonomous communities.

In 1539, on the eve of the Spanish arrival, tens of thousands of people were living in more than one hundred pueblos dotting the valley of the Rio Grande and its tributaries. The Pueblo world extended from northernmost Taos, south past Socorro to the Piro pueblos, west to Zuni, and east to the Salinas pueblos on the edge of the Great Plains. The latter cluster of as many as forty pueblos would be among the first to be abandoned during a century of violence that would envelope the entire Pueblo realm.

The Albuquerque area alone was home to at least a dozen villages. Here the people grew vast

An offering at the waterfall, Nambe, 1925
EDWARD S. CURTIS

gardens of melons, beans, corn, and other food crops. They domesticated turkeys, whose downy feathers they wove into warm robes, and grew cotton to make clothing and blankets. Nearby mountain ranges supplied ample game, fish, and wild foods.

Spanish explorers of 1581 provided a vivid description of the people they encountered at one pueblo, most likely Isleta:

"The men have their hair cut short, in the fashion of caps, so that they leave . . . on the crown of their heads, a sort of skull cap formed by their own hair. Others wear their hair long, to the shoulders, as the Indians of New Spain formerly did.

"Some adorn themselves with painted cotton pieces of cloth three spans long and two thirds wide, with which they cover their privy parts. Over this they wear, fastened at the shoulders, a blanket of the same material, painted with many long figures and colors. It reaches to their knees like the clothes of Mexicans. Some, in fact most of them, wear cotton skirts, hand painted and embroidered, that are very charming. They wear shoes.

"Below the waist the women wear cotton skirts, colored and embroidered, and above, a blanket of the same material like those used by the men. They wear it after the fashion of the Jewish women. They gird themselves over it with cotton sashes adorned with tassels. They comb their hair, which is long."

SPANISH CONTACT PERIOD

The world of the Pueblo peoples was forever altered in 1540 when Francisco Vásquez de Coronado led the first major Spanish expedition into what is now the United States in a vain search for the Seven Cities of Gold. He marched north from Mexico's Sea of Cortez across eastern Arizona, into the Rio Grande Valley of New Mexico, and spent a winter holed up in a pueblo near present-day Bernalillo.

Coronado and his men came seeking quick riches, like those his predecessors had found in Mexico, but instead they found a farming people with a highly evolved social, cultural, and religious life living in large, defensible villages of multistoried stone or adobe brick. The Spanish named them *Los Pueblos* (The Town People). But without easy plunder to be had, Spain was slow to establish a permanent presence in the Pueblo realm.

More than a generation would pass before Don Juan de Oñate would lead several hundred Hispanic settlers, soldiers, and a handful of Franciscan friars back to the Rio Grande Valley. The year was 1598, and the colonists were lured by the potential for agriculture and the opportunity to transform the town-dwelling inhabitants into good Catholics and subjects of the Spanish Crown. Near present-day Española, at San Juan Pueblo, they established the second permanent European colony in what is now the United States (the first having been founded in San Augustine, Florida, in 1565).

The Spanish Crown formally provided each pueblo with a perpetual land grant, and the Catholic Church recognized the people as human beings with souls. But, as Spanish subjects, the Pueblo peoples were obliged to pay taxes to the Crown in the form of food, hides, textiles, and manual labor. And as objects of Catholic missionary zeal, the Pueblo peoples were discouraged, often forcibly, from maintaining their traditional religious practices.

By the late 1600s, Hispanic settlements dotted the Rio Grande Valley, and the Pueblo peoples were reeling under the combined strictures of secular and religious authorities. In 1680, under the leadership of Popé of San Juan Pueblo, most of the pueblos rose in revolt, driving the Spanish out of New Mexico and killing about one thousand colonists in the process. Many priests were slain and churches were burned. In 1692, Don Diego de Vargas led an expedition up from El Paso to reassert Spanish control of New Mexico. After a two-year military campaign, he succeeded in bringing all of the rebellious pueblos back to the fold.

The two cultures settled into a relationship over the next two centuries that varied from wary to warm, with a great deal of cross-cultural exchange involving everything from food to language and genes. Pueblo and Spanish often fought side by side against common enemies, principally nomadic Navajo, Apache, Ute, and Comanche raiders. But the Spanish also inadvertently introduced diseases to which the Pueblo peoples had no immunity. Ensuing epidemics, coupled with attacks by the nomadic tribes and the loss of land and lifestyle, decimated the pueblos, and by the eighteenth century only nineteen major villages remained.

San Lorenzo Catholic church, Picuris
STEPHEN TRIMBLE

Turquoise necklace
by Mary Agnes Garcia, Santo Domingo
MARK NOHL

ANGLO-AMERICAN PERIOD

In 1846, the United States declared war on Mexico and troops under the command of General Stephen Watts Kearny occupied New Mexico. Two years later, with the signing of the Treaty of Guadalupe Hidalgo, the United States formally took possession of all Mexican territory north of the Gila River, and formally recognized the sovereignty, land base, and other rights of the various pueblos first codified by Spain and subsequently recognized by Mexico.

Even after the United States assumed control of New Mexico, the territory remained an isolated and dangerous place. Navajo, Ute, Apache, and Comanche raiders continued to plague Pueblo peoples, Hispanic settlers, and Anglo newcomers alike. The Civil War diverted attention and resources from the region, and not until war's end could the U.S. Army make an earnest effort to establish order. The capture of Geronimo, the legendary Apache leader, in 1886 marked the end of a long and bloody chapter.

Elimination of the "hostiles" and the arrival of the Atchison, Topeka, and Santa Fe Railway made New Mexico Territory more inviting for Anglo-American ranchers, miners, settlers, and merchants. The end of the nineteenth century saw the advent of large-scale ranching, industrial-scale mining, massive timber harvesting, and the founding of many towns. In the early twentieth century, artists and tourists "discovered" northern New Mexico. After World War I, the automobile industry boomed and the level of traffic to the region mushroomed. During World War II, the U.S. government located several important war-related installations in the state, not the least of which was the super-secret facility at Los Alamos. In the postwar era, high-tech manufacturing and computer science industries have become increasingly important to the state's economy.

While the federal government formally granted U.S. citizenship to the Pueblo peoples in 1924, the state of New Mexico did not extend them the same courtesy, or the right to vote in state elections, until 1948. Denied credit by banks and other financial institutions, Pueblo governments were mired in chronic poverty and struggled to provide for even the basic needs of their people, much less the infrastructure of modern communities, such as roads, telephone systems, schools, even clean drinking water and indoor toilets. Jobs on reservations were non-existent, and most adults after World War II began to work off reservation in a variety of fields. Education, employment, and income levels were among the worst in the nation, compounded by high incidences of alcoholism, mortality including youth suicide, and other social and health problems.

Contemporary Era

In the 1960s and 1970s, most pueblos began to assume control over many programs formerly administered by the federal government, in particular by the Department of Interior's Bureau of Indian Affairs.

In the 1980s, Indian gaming arrived on the scene, providing the first solid source of revenue for the eleven pueblos that have opened casinos. Profits from gaming are being invested in basic infrastructure, modern housing, new on-reservation enterprises, scholarship programs, health and fitness centers, and environmental projects. Gaming funds a wide range of public services including law enforcement, social services, job training, and elder care.

More and more Pueblo youth, including those from nongaming tribes, are pursuing a college education, and many graduates return home to work on tribal endeavors. Tribal governments also are becoming major players in the state's political and economic arenas.

As the pueblos reassert their sovereignty and strive to achieve economic independence, they are earning greater respect from their fellow New Mexicans, for New Mexico wouldn't be New Mexico without the Pueblo peoples and the invaluable contributions they have made, and continue to make, to our common culture.

San Geronimo Day, Taos, 1920
PHOTOGRAPHER UNKNOWN

Santo Domingo elder
STEPHEN TRIMBLE

Pueblo Customs

LANGUAGES

The various pueblos of New Mexico have in common certain customs, religious orientations and practices, arts, and social structures, but each of the nineteen pueblos remains an independent political entity. The Pueblo peoples also do not share a common language.

The Zuni people, for example, speak a language unique to that pueblo. Residents of the other pueblos speak Tewa, Tiwa, or Towa, all of which are related to the Azteco-Tanoan language group.

San Juan, Santa Clara, San Ildefonso, Pojoaque, Nambe, and Tesuque people speak Tewa. At Taos, Picuris, Sandia, and Isleta, residents speak Tiwa. Jemez is the only pueblo where Towa is spoken.

At Cochiti, Santo Domingo, San Felipe, Santa Ana, Zia, Laguna, and Acoma, the people speak Keres. This language is linguistically distinct from any other native to North America, which suggests that the ancestors of these Pueblo peoples may have been among the earliest to arrive in the Southwest.

COSMOLOGY

The Catholic Church has significantly influenced Pueblo culture since the mid-sixteenth century, when the Spanish arrived in New Mexico. Most Pueblo people are nominally Catholic, faithfully attending mass and using the church for baptism, confirmations, marriages and funerals. Yet native religion remains a powerful force, and ancient spiritual observances coexist with Catholic rites in a unique melding of faiths.

The religious pantheon of the Pueblos is far too complex to describe in detail here, but generally speaking the Pueblo peoples believe everything in the physical world has a spirit or force associated with it, and that life should be lived in harmony with these elements. Maintaining this balance, in one's own life and in the life of the people as a whole, is a spiritual imperative. Many dance ceremonies are a form of moving prayer, conducted to maintain this equilibrium, and the songs and dances serve as offerings to the spiritual forces that oversee all aspects of mortal life.

All of the Pueblos share a belief that mankind emerged into this world—the fifth world—from worlds below by climbing a tall ladder through a small hole in the sky. Many pueblos are divided into two main societies or moieties: the Winter People and the Summer People. Each of these groups maintains at least one kiva, or religious chamber, and is responsible for half the year's ceremonial cycle. Tall ladders that emerge from these kivas evoke the Emergence Story. Ancestral Pueblo kivas were typically located in round underground chambers. Contemporary kivas may be rectangular and located above ground. Kivas are sacred places and only Pueblo members are allowed to enter them. Young men are brought into the kivas for traditional teachings, which includes memorization of lengthy songs and chants that speak to the mysteries of the Pueblo spiritual cosmos.

SOCIAL BEHAVIOR AND CUSTOMS

Pueblo people are historically a peaceful people, who fought only when forced to. They prefer the gentle way, in voice, manner, and even handshake. Most Pueblo people prefer a light touch of the hands in greeting rather than the strong grasp of the typical "American" handshake.

Pueblo culture also is communitarian, stressing the good of the whole rather than the glory of the individual. Social behavior is governed by this code; standing out is considered poor form. One's personal success depends upon, and is a reflection of, the success of one's community. This is why "antique" artwork is unsigned, and even today most Pueblo people—artists included—are loathe to be singled out for attention or praise. This social code runs counter to the dominant culture's belief in the primacy of the individual, and its desire to recognize, celebrate, and reward exceptional works by gifted artists.

GOVERNMENTS

Authority in most pueblos is based upon a system instituted by the Spanish and continued with minor changes through the Mexican and American eras. Under this system, secular, day-to-day affairs and official business between a pueblo and the outside world—which includes county, state and federal governments—is handled by a governor, one or more lieutenant governors, an administrative staff, and a tribal court system. The governor is either directly elected by the pueblo's adult residents, or appointed by the tribal council. At some pueblos, the council is composed of former governors, while at others all adult males comprise the council. Only Isleta has had a female governor. Each pueblo also recognizes its religious authorities, including the caciques, who regulate and lead traditional religious activities, as well as war chiefs and assistant war chiefs.

In the early seventeenth century, the Spanish Crown presented wooden canes with silver caps to each Pueblo to be used by that community's governor as a symbol of his authority. In 1863, President Abraham Lincoln provided the Pueblos with another set of canes to memorialize federal recognition of the Pueblos as sovereign nations—arguably the oldest in continual existence in America. These canes are imbued with powerful social significance and are handled with great ceremony by Pueblo authorities today.

Art, Crafts, and Culture

The Pueblo people are recognized as some of the world's most gifted artists, a remarkable achievement considering they have no word for art in their own languages. Artistic expression always has been part of the fabric of daily life. Before the twentieth century, artists rarely, if ever, signed their works of art, and the objects they produced were considered no more significant or valuable than a well-planted seed or a well-said prayer.

But today Pueblo art is big business. Collectors from around the world visit New Mexico to acquire the latest creations by their favorite Pueblo artists. Individuals, entire families—and in the case of Zuni, the entire pueblo—depend upon the income derived from the production of various arts and crafts.

The emergence of a thriving market for Pueblo works of art has encouraged Pueblo peoples to retain ancient cultural and artistic traditions that might otherwise have been overwhelmed by the dominant culture. This market also has enabled Pueblo artisans to earn a living close to home. And with the support of eager buyers and collectors,

Pueblo arts have entered a "golden age" characterized by the finest workmanship in both traditional and contemporary media.

Unfortunately, the popularity of Pueblo art objects has attracted its share of charlatans and fast-buck artists, who regard Pueblo arts and culture as mere commodities to be exploited. Legitimate Pueblo artists bemoan the flood of fraudulent Indian-style arts and crafts produced by both foreign and domestic sources. Their best defense is an informed public: buyers who insist on purchasing only authentic Pueblo works of art.

POTTERY

Pueblo artisans are perhaps best known for exquisite pottery. Pottery making in this region is believed to have arisen circa A.D. 200-300, most likely from the practice of lining baskets with clay. In the past, work was produced for cooking, storage of foods, carrying water and so forth, but today pottery making has become a fine art, with an astounding range of forms and decorative styles.

The most common forms include pots and vases of many styles—including seed pots with their tiny mouths and wedding vases with their entwined necks—and sizes ranging from four-foot ollas to one-inch miniatures. Also popular are plates, and animal and human figurines, including storytellers—whimsical, open-mouthed figures piled up with children. Potters also produce oddities such as candlesticks, canteens, ladles, salt and pepper shakers, clay jewelry, smoking devices, even Christmas tree ornaments and Nativity scenes. Practical as well as creative, Pueblo potters, generally women, have modified and continue to modify traditional pottery forms based upon sales success or failure.

Decorative coloration ranges from the lustrous black-on-black to redware, black-on-white, or polychrome—mixtures of various shades of red, brown, buffs, cream, black, and other earthy colors. The colors are achieved with either natural clay tones used as the base material, with liquid slips that are painted on, or with application of mineral or vegetal paints—such as a rich blackish-green made from wild spinach. The pueblos of Nambe, Picuris, and Taos are also noted for their use of clay flecked with mica that produces a glittery surface in a bronze, gold, or orange color. Such work, called micaceous pottery, is left unpainted in its natural state of beauty.

Textures can include a smooth and highly polished finish to works that are deeply incised or lightly scribed when the clay is still damp, or a combination of these styles. Design elements can range from falling-rain patterns, flowers, birds, clouds, spirals, and other pictorial motifs drawn from nature or the supernatural (for example, the horned water serpent often found on San Ildefonso work) to purely geometric work—as in the fine-line style of Acoma or the blockier geometrics typical of Santo Domingo pottery.

Most famous for their pottery are artisans of Santa Clara and San Ildefonso, with their beautiful blackwear and redwares, and Acoma. But every pueblo has its potters. And while certain pueblos have definable styles, much borrowing and mixing of styles is now common. Cochiti is best known for its production of storytellers, but Acoma also produces them and other pueblos are taking them up as well. Several Jemez potters produce another clay figurine—the so-called Corn Mothers.

The demand for pottery vessels has grown so great that some artisans—especially at Acoma—are purchasing unfinished pottery called "greenware," "ceramic-style," or "contemporary style" that is cast from a liquid clay. These manufactured goods are then hand painted and fired in gas kilns, often producing a work with a high sheen. If you seek a work that has been traditionally made, ask the artist or salesperson about the process used.

A traditional work of pottery involves a complex process that includes gathering the clay from the land, preparing it (which involves sorting, grinding, sifting, mixing with a binder, and soaking), building the work by use of clay coils, smoothing it, allowing it to dry, sanding it, applying the surface color and finishing design to it, and then baking it outdoors in a wood fire. This explains the cost associated with traditional pottery, which often shocks first-time buyers. It is a difficult and time-consuming process, which can be ruined during the last step by a firing accident.

right: (clockwise from top) San Ildefonso storage jar, 1918; Zia pot, 1890; Santa Anna water jar, pre-1926; Acoma seed jar, pre-1925; Santo Domingo pot, 1915
MARK NOHL

JEWELRY

Jewelry is another of the major Pueblo arts, almost on a par with pottery. As long as rivers have run, people of the region have adorned themselves with forms of jewelry—a shell tied with yucca string around the neck, a pretty stone held around the wrist. Long ago quite sophisticated techniques were in use. In fact, an excavation at Chaco Canyon uncovered a necklace of some twenty-five hundred finely worked turquoise beads created circa A.D. 1200.

However, introduction of silver casting techniques by the Spanish ushered in a major evolutionary step in regional Indian jewelry making. The Navajo are believed to have first acquired silversmithing expertise during their internment at Bosque Redondo in the 1860s, and thereafter passed on this knowledge to a few Zuni and Hopi artisans. Improvements in creating heishi—tiny beads of shell or stone—and the cutting and finishing of other stones and shell followed. (The word *heishi* is derived from the Keres word for "shell.") These improvements, combined with the new metalsmithing processes and the development of new markets brought by the railroad and then the automobile, led to a dramatic expansion of Pueblo jewelry artistry in the twentieth century, particularly after the 1960s.

The range of materials used and the forms created are now as diverse as the colors of a rainbow. Along with the always popular blue turquoise and red coral, jewelers today are using such exotic materials as Afghani lapis lazuli, Siberian charoite,

Cippy Crazyhorse, jeweler, Cochiti
MARK NOHL

*left: Turquoise and spiny oyster shell necklace
by Mary Agnes Garcia, Santo Domingo*
MARK NOHL

Australian opal, spiny oyster shell, petrified wood and ivory, jasper, sugilite, mother of pearl, jet, abalone, ironwood, agate, and even diamonds. Supplementing sterling silver are works set in gold. Besides traditional necklaces (a diverse class in itself), bracelets, earrings and rings, today one can purchase money clips, belt buckles, lighters, hair clips, pendants, pins, and many other forms of jewelry.

Along with the diversification of materials and forms have come new processes. In addition to traditional sandcasting, artists are employing other fabrication techniques including lost-wax casting, tufa casting, and sheet silver working. The latter can involve cutting and shaping, hammering, and soldering work into its basic shape, then applying texture through use of custom-made stamps, appliqué and repoussé techniques, and the setting of stones. Also common nowadays is the overlay technique, first popularized by the Hopi in the 1940s. In this process, a design is cut from a sheet of silver. The sheet is then soldered over another layer of silver, which is darkened through an oxidation process, creating a dramatic two-dimensional design surface.

As with pottery, almost every pueblo has jewelers at work, but certain pueblos are noted for particular styles of jewelry design. Zuni—the major source for Pueblo jewelry as a whole—is renowned for the artisans' use of settings composed of lots of small turquoise stones (as in the cluster and needlepoint styles), and for mosaic and inlay work in a variety of stone and shell. Santo Domingo—the second greatest source of Pueblo jewelry today—was the historic center for production of heishi. Today the pueblo's artisans still produce a lot of fine beads, which require laborious hand cutting and grinding.

PAINTING

Forms of painting—pictographs made with mineral paints applied to rock surfaces, petroglyphs made by pecking images into rock surfaces, and images on plaster, as in the prehistoric kivas of Coronado State Monument—have been practiced in the region for eons, but the development of painting and other works on paper by Pueblo artists only evolved in the twentieth century. Their outstanding design sensibilities, however, allowed them to quickly master these media as well.

Students of Dorothy Dunn at the Santa Fe Indian School in the 1930s sparked the first outpouring of Pueblo visual arts, and works by leading artists of that era—including Jose Rey Toledo, Ben Quintana, Joe Herrera, Pablita Velarde, Allan Houser, Velino Herrera, and Pop Chalee—are now highly sought after. In 1962 the Institute of American Indian Arts was launched in Santa Fe and quickly began to produce the next generation of outstanding contemporary Native artists drawn from Indian reservations throughout the nation, including many pueblos.

Today painters are working at many of the pueblos, particularly Zuni but also Zia, San Ildefonso, San Juan, Tesuque, Isleta, and Santa Clara.

SCULPTURE

Traditional Pueblo sculpture included the carving of wood and stone fetishes and katsina (kachina) dolls. Katsina dolls are small (six inches to two feet tall), three-dimensional images of various Pueblo deities. They were used historically to instruct Pueblo children about the Pueblo pantheon and to serve as reminders of the eternal presence of the katsinam in pueblo homes. Today, carving authentic katsina dolls for commercial sale is almost exclusively a Hopi art form. A few Zuni artists produce katsinas for sale, but as a general rule New Mexico Pueblo artisans do not create katsina dolls.

Fetishes are carved images of animals, and traditionally the "feeding" and care of these figurines was thought to endow one with their characteristics. The Zunis produce the vast majority of fetishes today, which can come as miniatures strung as necklaces, or as small, freestanding forms.

Other Pueblo artisans are also making fetishes today, some as large as four feet in length, which should really be considered a true sculptural form rather than a fetish.

In addition, dozens of Pueblo artisans are working in contemporary sculptural media, including bronze, monumental forms, and fabricated works in steel and stone.

TEXTILE ARTS

In the prehistoric and early historic eras, the Pueblos produced a great volume of woven goods from cotton they cultivated (as well as unique winter coats made from layers of feathers plucked from domesticated turkeys). In fact, the Spanish often collected blankets as a form of tax imposed on the Pueblos. However, the Navajos are now the renowned Native weavers of the region—regarded among the very best in the world. Aside from belts—usually of white cotton with black, green, and red elements—and similarly decorated kilts, the Pueblos produce few or no woven goods. Decorative embroidery is still practiced widely, however. For woven goods and embroidery, visit Nambe, Santa Clara, Tesuque, San Juan, Laguna, Acoma, or Zuni.

OTHER ARTS AND CRAFTS

Pueblo artisans are busy working in other fields as well. While leather crafts are not widely pursued these days, Cochiti is a renowned center for the production of traditional Pueblo-style drums, and a few drummakers can also be found at Taos and Tesuque. Traditional moccasins, wonderfully comfortable and durable, can be found at Taos and a few other pueblos. Quivers, wrist bow guards, and other leather goods are also made here and there.

Basketmaking is another Pueblo craft that is largely absent today. The Hopi (as well as other Arizona tribes) continue this practice, but Jemez is one of the few New Mexico pueblos whose artists produce plaited yucca works. Some willow baskets are also made at Santo Domingo. Zia, Acoma, and Sandia also have several working basketmakers.

right: Corn dancers, Jemez, 1935
T. HARMON PARKHURST

In addition to these arts, Pueblo artisans are working in media including glass, photography (see Taos or Laguna chapters), film, printmaking, papermaking (see Zuni), and myriad novel forms.

Note: Many of the most renowned Pueblo artists and craftspeople do not show or sell their work within their home pueblos. They tend to show their works in leading galleries in Santa Fe, Albuquerque, Taos, and other art centers throughout the region and nation. However, many excellent artists—particularly potters and jewelers—do sell their work from home studios. In addition to getting a better price than you would at a commercial gallery, all income goes directly to the artist.

Etiquette

Pueblo people are generally very hospitable and welcome visitors, but keep the following suggestions in mind to avoid misunderstandings or violations of customs.

Remember, the pueblos are sovereign nations administered by tribal governments. Pueblo villages are places of residence, work, and worship. Nonresidents are guests of the various tribal governments and the pueblo residents, and should behave accordingly.

Failure to abide by the following guidelines could result in expulsion from a pueblo, a possible fine and/or legal action, and possible closure of a pueblo to all visitors.

General

Never enter a home without permission, unless a sign identifies the residence as an art gallery or studio.

Never enter a kiva, which is a ceremonial place of worship open to residents only.

Do not enter cemeteries.

Stay in the immediate area of the village center. Many areas outside of the village core are considered sacred and are not to be disturbed.

Do not climb on structures.

Observe posted restrictions or physical barriers erected to keep visitors out of certain areas.

Most pueblos are occasionally closed to all visitors, in which case roads will be blocked. Do not attempt to enter the reservations at these times.

Do not remove pottery sherds or other artifacts found on the reservation.

Alcohol, drugs, and weapons are not allowed on the reservations.

Do not bring pets into the pueblo villages.

Drive slowly.

Do not litter.

Ceremonial

Ceremonial dances are sacred enactments, not a form of entertainment or amusement. Do not clap following a dance or throw money at the dance group. Your appreciation is best shown by silence.

Do not distract the dancers by talking, waving to friends, or otherwise calling attention to yourself.

Do not touch the dancers or attempt to talk to them, not even to say hello to someone you know.

Do not ask questions about the meaning of the dance being enacted.

Children must be kept quiet and under strict control at all times.

Unless you are specifically invited to take a seat, do not sit on chairs that may be set up around the dance area. They belong to pueblo residents.

You may notice that some people observe the dances from the rooftops. They are there by invitation only.

Try not to obstruct your neighbors' view of the dance.

If you are invited to dine with a resident family on a feast day, politely accept. But realize that the same family may extend the same invitation to many visitors, and thus may have many guests to serve. Others may be waiting to take your place at the table, so do not linger.

PHOTOGRAPHY

Each pueblo has its own regulations regarding still and video photography. Most require a permit and forbid photography of ceremonies. Some pueblos also forbid photos of their kivas, cemeteries, and church interiors. If you break these rules, your film and/or camera may be confiscated, you may be expelled from the pueblo, and you may be fined or prosecuted.

Most masses at pueblo Catholic churches are open to the public. Behave appropriately.

Authorization for photography is intended for personal use only. Most pueblos have special fees and regulations for photography intended for commercial use. Please check first.

If you wish to photograph an individual, ask their permission first. A photo permit does not automatically grant you this right. Some "models" may request a small cash fee.

If a pueblo does allow photography of a ceremony, do so in an unobtrusive manner. Do not enter the dance area, block the entrance or progress of the dancers or singers, or obstruct the view of other spectators.

ACOMA

(AH-koh-ma)

Hak'u: "To Prepare or Plan"

ALL NINETEEN NEW MEXICO PUEBLOS are in scenic locations, but none surpasses Acoma's picturesque setting atop a 376-foot-high sandstone butte. From the heights of Acoma, aptly nicknamed "Sky City," one is eye-level with passing hawks and clouds. Great vistas open on all sides of other massive buttes, rock-walled canyons, and, to the north, the looming profile of Mount Taylor.

Until the early twentieth century, Acoma remained accessible only by a rough foot trail, and the residents of this impregnable mesa-top community fiercely resisted acculturation. Today, the people of Acoma welcome visitors to their Sky City and many tribal members earn their living as master potters. You can purchase pottery directly from the artisans, or perhaps grab a loaf of their wonderful bread baked in beehive-shaped, wood-fired, outdoor ovens called hornos.

Acoma Pueblo consists of rows of centuries-old, two- and three-story adobe buildings that intentionally lack electricity and running water. Sky City is a designated National Historic Landmark.

Attending a dance here is a memorable experience. The dancers and singers emerge from the kiva, descend tall ladders, and make their way to the small central plaza. Visitors and residents crowd the space to experience the spectacle; many gaze down from

left: Historic foot trail to Sky City, Acoma
STEPHEN TRIMBLE

surrounding rooftops. The drummer begins the cadence and the steady thumping of feet resounds off the earth, complemented by the percussive sound of rattles and bells tied to the dancers' limbs.

History

Pot by Marie Chino Grace, Acoma
MARK NOHL

Acoma, Taos, and old Orabi of the Hopi reservation in Arizona vie for bragging rights as America's oldest continually inhabited locale. Acoma was established at or near its present location as early as A.D. 900, and Sky City may have been occupied since 1075, although some sources suggest 1150.

The Spanish conquistadors viewed the site as a superb defensive location and initially avoided military confrontation. Francisco Vásquez de Coronado visited Acoma in 1540 and became the first non-Native to enter Sky City. "The ascent was so difficult we repented climbing to the top," he wrote. "The houses stand three and four stories high. The people . . . have abundant supplies of maize (corn), beans, and turkeys. . . ."

However, in January 1599, Don Juan de Oñate ordered seventy Spanish soldiers to attack the fortress in retaliation for the death of his nephew and ten other Spaniards. Over the course of three days, these soldiers succeeded in mounting the mesa by a log bridge from an adjoining mesa. With cannon and hand arms, they killed a thousand defenders and took the pueblo. Many people

Acoma, 1883

BEN WITTICK

jumped from the cliffs or ran into burning buildings rather than surrender. Afterward, the Spanish hacked off one foot each from all Acoma males older than twenty-five years of age, and sent the younger males and females to Mexico as slaves.

The injustice of this tragic incident still burns in the hearts of the people of Acoma. It was not an easy path for their ancestors to learn to live with the Spanish. Guides at the pueblo today will mention that, in the years following their capitulation, the people of Acoma occasionally rose up and gave offending Catholic priests "flying lessons" off the mesa.

Life did not change much with the occupation of New Mexico by the United States in 1846. The pueblo's population continued to decline, and by 1900 only five hundred residents remained. Ironically, it was Hollywood that helped spur the pueblo's revival and facilitate greater public access. In the mid-1940s, filmmakers came to shoot a movie and bulldozed a road to the mesa top that is still in use today.

Contemporary Life

In 1982, Acoma became one of the first pueblos to establish a gaming enterprise with a high-stakes bingo parlor. Today this business has grown into a major casino-hotel complex operated alongside I-40 that attracts truckers and other travelers. With this income the tribe has launched a Keresan language program (the pueblo's native language) and a historical preservation program, is building a public safety facility housing a fire

station and police center, and has begun many other endeavors. They have also purchased several nearby ranches to add to the 400,000 acres within their large reservation, which support several thousand head of cattle. A traditionally appointed governor and tribal council lead Acoma's secular government.

Most Acoma residents, numbering just over six thousand, live off Sky City mesa in one of three villages—Acomita, McCarty, and Anzac—along the Rio San Jose, a tributary of the Rio Grande. Particularly beautiful are the stone Santa Maria Mission at McCarty, and the adobe Saint Ann's Mission at Acomita. Only thirty or so people— mostly elders—still reside fulltime in Sky City, but most families still maintain homes on the mesa top, which they occupy during the pueblo's many multi-day ceremonies.

Art, Crafts, and Culture

Acoma is home to an active artistic community and is a primary Pueblo pottery center. Perhaps the most distinctive style of its pottery artisans is the "fine-line" form composed of delicate geometric designs carefully applied by hand on the vessels' exterior—often black lines over a white base. Artists such as Dorothy Torivio, Rebecca Lewis Lucario, Dorothy Sanchez, and Carolyn Lewis Concho have taken this style to new heights.

But Acoma artists are bold, and have jumped into a diverse array of pottery styles and forms, producing storytellers, polychrome work, small-mouthed seed pots, vessels with naturalistic and animal design elements, and Christmas tree ornaments. They even work with purple coloration and employ other novel finishes, such as the "horsehair"

style. In this process, horsehair is dropped on a vessel's off-white surface after it has been heated, creating swirling black line patterns. Charmae Nateway produces square vessels, while Wilfred Garcia creates all-white goods.

Also popular at Acoma are animal designs adopted from prehistoric pottery produced by the

ACOMA

Must-see: Sky City, San Estevan Mission, vendors, views

〰〰〰

All events at Sky City, unless otherwise indicated. Call for details.

early February: Governor's Feast

March/April:
Easter mass in Acomita and McCarty

May (first Sunday):
Santa Maria Feast Day at McCarty

June 24: San Juan Day events

June 29: San Pedro y San Paulo Day events

July 10-13: *Pueblo is closed annually*

July 25: Santiago Day events

August 10: San Lorenzo Feast Day
in Acomita

September 2: San Estevan Feast Day
(Acoma's primary annual event)
with various dances

October: *Pueblo is closed annually
on the first or second weekend*

December 24: lighting of thousands of
luminarias and evening mass at San Estevan

December 25-28: various dances

〰〰〰

P.O. Box 309, Acoma, NM 87034
(800) 747-0181 or (505) 552-6017

VISITING ACOMA

DIRECTIONS: To reach Acoma from **Albuquerque**, head west on I-40 for 55 miles to Exit 108 and proceed south on Tribal Road 23 for 11 miles to the Visitor Center. From Grants, head east on I-40 for 19 miles to Exit 102 and head south 14 miles on Tribal Roads 30 and 32 to the Visitor Center.

VISITOR CENTER/MUSEUM: Acoma has two visitor facilities—the **Acoma/ Route 66 Interpretive Center** and the **Sky City Visitor Center**. The latter also houses exhibits about Acoma's colorful history, historic photos, a snack bar, restrooms, and a gift shop with books, CDs and tapes, a little jewelry, Pendleton blankets, T-shirts, and souvenirs. Open daily, Apr.–Oct. daily 8 A.M.–7 P.M.; Nov.–Mar. 8 A.M.–4:30 P.M.

TOURS: The only way to visit the historic village of **Sky City** is to take a guided tour, which departs from the visitor center. You are bused to the mesa top, where a guide will meet you for the approximate one-hour walking tour. If you're in decent shape, allow extra time for the optional descent down the old foot trail. Tours operate daily Apr.–Oct. 8 A.M.–6 P.M., and Nov.–Mar. 8 A.M.–3:30 P.M. Due to tribal ceremonies, tours are not held July 10–13, and the first or second weekend of October. Tours cost $9 for adults, $8 for seniors, $6 for children six to seventeen. (800) 747-0181 or (505) 469-1052.

PHOTOGRAPHY: A still-camera permit is $10, available at the Visitor Center. Video cameras are forbidden. No photography is allowed inside San Esteban or the cemetery.

SKETCHING/SOUND RECORDING: Not allowed.

CASINO: The **Sky City Casino** is open 24 hours every day of the year. Exit 102 off I-40. (888) SKY-CITY

DINING: The **Sky City Visitor Center** has a snack bar. The **Huwak'a Restaurant**, in the **Sky City Casino**, has a wonderful buffet open for breakfast, lunch, and dinner located in a room separate from gaming activities, featuring tile floors and Acoma art.

ACCOMMODATIONS: The luxurious **Sky City Hotel**, attached to the casino, opened in early 2001 with 150 rooms, pool, workout room, and Jacuzzi.

CAMPING: No facilities, although a tent and RV campground is planned.

RECREATION: For catfish and rainbow trout fishing, visit **Acomita Lake**. Tackle, bait, and snacks are found at a convenience center. The lake is open Apr.–Nov., dawn to dusk, just off Exit 100 south of the highway. A one-day permit is $6. (505) 552-9866.

The tribe also conducts five-day, guided trophy **elk hunts** in September and October. Call (505) 552-6968.

Climbing on the reservation's impressive rock formations is forbidden. Hiking is not allowed.

ARTISTS AND GALLERIES: Many artists sell their pottery, jewelry, and baked goods from tables set up daily atop **Sky City mesa**. The annual feast day on September 2 brings out almost every artist. Among the many artists selling at Sky City are **Dorothy Sanchez**, who produces award-winning fine-line-style pottery, (505) 552-9546; and **Gertrude Ann Romero**, who works in traditional and ceramic forms, including Christmas tree ornaments, (505) 552-9491. **Irvin Louis** and the **Yellow Corn Shop** offer carved horsehair-style bowls and wedding vases, (505) 839-2589; **Isidore** and **Frances Concho** make traditional pottery, (505) 552-6788; and **Susan Sarracino** creates traditional and contemporary pottery, including some striking blue works, (505) 552-7471.

Other Acoma artisans sell work in the **Sky City Visitor Center parking lot**. Notable here is the shop-on-wheels of **Joseph Salvador**, (505) 552-7305. Tucked into a small van is a working jewelry studio and display cases of his fine jewelry, including stamped silver work and beaded necklaces. Also selling in the parking area is **Clara Santiago**, who makes hand-painted traditional and etched ceramic Christmas ornaments, quail and turtle figurines, and miniature pots, (505) 552-7308.

Other outstanding Acoma potters include **Mary Lewis Garcia**, a daughter of famed potter **Lucy Lewis**. Mary works in traditional forms and materials,

gathering her own clay and producing handsome polychrome vessels. Box 467, #192, Acoma Pueblo, NM 87034-0467; (505) 552-9692.

Sharon and **Bernard Lewis** produce fine, small vessels with detailed drawings of lizards and geometric patterns in colored slips over a white base. (505) 552-0361.

Potters **Marietta** and **Melvin Juanico** work in the eye-dazzling "fine line" geometric pattern school. (505) 552-6285, or e-mail at MPJ111 @aol.com.

Pueblo Pottery Gallery owners **Arthur and Carol Cruz** carry a wide selection of pottery by many of Acoma's most renowned artisans, as well as by artists from Santa Clara, San Ildefonso, San Juan, Jemez, Cochiti, and other pueblos. They also offer an assortment of Navajo rugs, katsina dolls, Zuni fetishes, and other work. Located in Acomita on Tribal Road 30, four miles south of Exit 102 off I-40. (800) 933-5771, (505) 552-6748, or www.pueblopotterygallery.com. Open Tues.–Sat. 9 A.M.–6 P.M. and Sun. 11 A.M.–6 P.M.

The **Acoma/Route 66 Interpretive Center** is an attractive facility opened in March 2000 with excellent historic displays about famed Route 66, America's first transcontinental highway. The center also has historic photos of Acoma and displays outstanding pottery. Its gift shop carries a selection of arts and crafts, including carved pottery, soft dolls, Acoma T-shirts, books on regional subjects, jewelry (especially earrings, including some made from clay), and Pueblo dried food products. Located next to the **Sky City Casino**, Exit 102 off I-40.

The **Sky City Casino Gift Shop** offers an excellent selection of Acoma pottery and jewelry.

Jake's Acoma Bakery features old-fashioned horno-baked bread, as well as conventionally baked bread, sweet rolls, cookies, fruit pies, and other goods produced by **Jacob and Mabel Vallo**. On Fridays all goods are in stock. Homemade tamales, as well as some jewelry (mostly Navajo and Zuni), woven shoulder bags and traditional sashes, and Navajo sandpaintings are also available. Located on Tribal Road 30 just south of the Administration Building. (505) 552-9292. Open Tues.–Fri. 8 A.M.–5 P.M.

Cornfield and Mt. Taylor, Acoma
STEPHEN TRIMBLE

Mimbres culture, and vessels with a "corrugated" surface texture of deliberately rough lines.

Some Acoma potters, as well as potters at other pueblos, fire their works in gas kilns today versus the traditional outdoor wood firing. This provides a more controlled process and consistent result, and does not necessarily alter the look of the finished product, but if you want a work of all-traditional pottery, ask about the process used.

Other Acoma potters are also buying or making slip-cast pottery, in which liquid clay is poured into a mold and then dried and decorated. Called *contemporary style, greenware,* or *ceramic-style,* it is functional and can be attractive, but can't be considered authentically traditional.

Many Acoma artists also work in jewelry, and there is some weaving of belts and some artisans producing baskets.

While the Acoma people continue to vigorously maintain their traditional religious practices, Sky City is also home to one of the nation's more remarkable Catholic churches, San Estevan del Rey Mission. Construction began in 1629 by Acoma laborers under the direction of Franciscan friar Juan

Ramirez and was finished in 1640. It is believed that as many as 168 men and women died building the church, which required twenty thousand tons of earth and water to be hauled up the old foot trail to make the adobe bricks. The original ceiling beams were harvested on Mount Taylor, some thirty miles away, and carried overland by teams of men who were forbidden to rest the beams on the ground at any time.

The massive structure—with a seventy-foot-high ceiling supported by the original corbels (the beams have been replaced) and adobe walls measuring ten feet thick at their base—is awesomely simple in its decor, with dirt floors and no pews. The altar features a large carved, wood image of San Estevan, and four spiral posts representing candles and the four cardinal directions. A statue of San Juan is found in a niche to the right and a ceiling panel contains images of the sun and moon. The church is part of the larger mission complex, which covers twenty-one thousand square feet in all. Pueblo authorities are planning to restore the entire mission, an ambitious and expensive undertaking.

COCHITI

(KOH-chee-tee)

Katyete or Ko-chits: "Stone Kiva"

ABOUT EIGHT CENTURIES AGO, ancestors of the Cochiti people settled down at an idyllic spot on the west bank of the Rio Grande in northern New Mexico. Here the mighty Rio Grande exits the confines of narrow White Rock Canyon, slows down, and spreads out as it enters a broad valley. Meandering through this rich alluvial plain, the river is lined with forests of massive, gnarled cottonwoods.

Over the centuries, the resourceful people of Cochiti created an elaborate network of acequias, or irrigation ditches, that direct life-sustaining water from the mother river to thirsty fields of alfalfa, corn, beans, squash, and fruit trees. Construction of a massive dam across the Rio Grande in the 1970s, just upstream from the pueblo, seemed like a good idea at the time, but Cochiti today must deal with the unexpected environmental and social consequences of that project.

A more positive development is the creation of a new national monument, Tent Rocks, on the western boundary of the Cochiti reservation, on sacred lands the pueblo historically controlled. Tribal authorities and the National Park Service will jointly manage the new monument. The pueblo is also constructing a multipurpose youth center dedicated to the physical, mental, social, and spiritual health of the pueblo's young people.

Today, Cochiti is noted for its artists, particularly potters who make storytellers and figurines, and its eighteen-hole golf course.

Retiring and protective of their traditions and privacy, the people of Cochiti nevertheless are among the friendliest of the state's nineteen pueblos, welcoming visitors to timeless dance rituals conducted in their simple plaza.

History

The Cochiti people are the northernmost speakers of the Keres language group. Their oral history tells of an ancient place called White House, where they lived following their emergence into this world. Eventually, they migrated south and east to the Jemez Mountains, where they settled in small villages in canyons of the Pajarito Plateau overlooking the Rio Grande's White Rock Canyon. Perhaps as early as A.D. 1225, they established the foundations of today's pueblo village on the west bank of the Rio Grande below White Rock Canyon. This would make Cochiti one of the oldest continually inhabited sites in North America, and the oldest of the pueblos in the central Rio Grande Valley.

Deer dancer figurine by Louis Naranjo, Cochiti
MARK NOHL

right: Corn dancers, Cochiti, 1934
T. HARMON PARKHURST

When the Rodriquez-Chamuscado expedition moved through the area in 1581, the Spanish explorers found a village of some 230 homes clustered in a block two and three stories tall. While initial relations with the Spanish were cordial, they soured over time, and the Cochiti people actively participated in the Pueblo Revolt of 1680. When

Don Diego de Vargas led the Spanish re-conquest of the area in 1692, he discovered that the Cochiti people, as well as members of San Felipe and Santo Domingo pueblos, had taken refuge in a fortified pueblo on Potrero Viejo, a high mesa north of Cochiti. Vargas laid siege, then successfully talked the Pueblo people into returning peacefully to

VISITING COCHITI

DIRECTIONS: Located in the **Rio Grande Valley** 43 miles north of **Albuquerque** and 38 miles southwest of **Santa Fe**. To get there from **Santa Fe**, head south on I-25 about eighteen miles to Exit 264. Proceed 8.5 miles west on NM 16 to the intersection with NM 22, and then turn north (right). Continue 2.5 miles to BIA 84, at the foot of the dam just west of the river. Turn south (left) and proceed 3 miles to the village's fifth entrance road on the left, Cochiti Street. The Governor's Office, a yellow stucco structure, is located on the left just past the Head Start building.

From **Albuquerque**, head north on I-25 to Exit 259 and then northwest on NM 22 through the Hispanic village of Peña Blanca to the dam. From there, follow directions as from Santa Fe.

VISITOR CENTER/MUSEUM: No tribal visitor center, although one is proposed for **Tent Rocks National Monument** adjoining the reservation. The Army Corps of Engineers, which oversees operation of **Cochiti Dam**, runs a small but informative **visitor center** overlooking the lake. Exhibits describe local geology, fauna, and flora (including medicinal plants, native foods, and craft plants), history, and the arts and lifeways of Cochiti Pueblo. It also has detailed dioramas of the **Rio Grande** and **Jemez Mountains**. Public restrooms are available in the visitor center. Open weekdays 8:30 A.M.–3:30 P.M., Sat. 10 A.M.–2 P.M., Sunday noon–4 P.M. Closed on Thanksgiving, Christmas, New Year's Day.

TOURS: None.

PHOTOGRAPHY: Not allowed.

SKETCHING/SOUND RECORDING: Not allowed.

DINING: A restaurant in the clubhouse of the **Pueblo de Cochiti Golf Course**

serves simple breakfasts and lunches, as well as fresh pizza and beer. A convenience store in the small town of Cochiti carries pizza and deli and snack items. (505) 465-2239.

ACCOMMODATIONS: None at the pueblo, but easily available in **Albuquerque** and **Santa Fe**.

CAMPING: The Army Corps of Engineers operates campgrounds and restrooms on the west shore of **Cochiti Lake** that are open year round. Camping is also available on the east side of the Rio Grande at the **Tetilla Peak Recreation Area** Apr. 1–Oct. 31. RV spaces with full electric hookups cost $12 per night, and tent sites are $7. Closed on Thanksgiving, Christmas, and New Year's Day. Information: (505) 465-0307. Reservations: (877) 444-6777.

RECREATION: **Cochiti Dam** created a large reservoir that backs up into the lower reaches of **White Rock Canyon** and provides opportunities for no-wake boating, swimming, and fishing. Information: (505) 465-0307. Marina: (505) 465-2219.

Tent Rocks National Monument, located on federal lands along Cochiti's west border, is a terrific place for an easy walk in splendid scenery. Turn off BIA 84 at the main village, go 1/3 mile south of Pueblo Road, onto Forest Road 226 and proceed 4.5 miles to the site. It is open Nov. 1–Mar. 31 from 8 A.M.– 5 P.M. and Apr. 1–Oct. 31 from 7 A.M.– 6 P.M. All-terrain vehicles are not allowed. Entry fee is $5 per vehicle. (505) 761-8704.

ARTISTS AND GALLERIES: **Steve Herrera's** home studio is located east of the Governor's Office. Look for the family name on the front fence. The pueblo's most renowned drummaker, Herrera produces a wide range of instruments, including purely ceremonial

drums with a black band on the top rim. Open year round but call first, (505) 465-2349. At the same address, **Nadine Pecos** produces miniature father and mother storytellers and nativity scenes. She collects her own clay, uses acrylic paints, and fires her figures in a gas kiln. (505) 465-2855.

Arnold Herrera is both a master drummaker and a talented jeweler. His sons—**Tim**, **Carlos** and **Tomas**— are following him into drummaking. (505) 473-4352.

Salvador and **Wilson Romero** are noted stone carvers and fetish artisans. The works are available at **Keshi of Santa Fe**, (505) 989-8728.

Felicita Eustace is a talented story-teller maker and jeweler. Among her daughters are jewelers **Christine**, **Jolene**, and **Bernadette**. Grandson **James Eustace** also creates delicate silver leaves highlighted with a colorful variety of worked stones. (505) 465-0399.

Cippy Crazyhorse works almost exclusively in pure silver, creating elegant designs that he chisels and stamps into bracelets, belt buckles, conchos, and handmade beads. His designs derive from a wide variety of hand punches he makes himself. Patrons include the **Heard Museum gift shop** of Phoenix and **Four Winds Gallery** in Pittsburgh. His studio is located on Cedar Road (look for the old "Cochiti Curio Shop" sign). Studio: (505) 465-2375; home: (505) 465-2549, www.crazyhorse.ws.

Other famous Cochiti artists past and present include storyteller artisans Seferina Ortiz, Maria Romero, G.R. Lovato, Mary and Leonard Trujillo, Mary Anderson, Snowflake Cordero (Rhodes), Nadine and Trinnie Herrera, Ramona Herrera, Dorothy Herrera, Ada Suina, and Joanne Trujillo. To learn more about them and the availability of their work, contact the Governor's Office.

their villages. In a second rebellion of 1696, Vargas returned to the site and met stiff resistance. He stormed the mesa top and defeated the rebels, led by Lucas Naranjo, who was beheaded.

In the 1680s and 1690s, some Cochiti people left the village to establish Laguna pueblo with refugees of other pueblos.

Contemporary Life

In the early 1970s, the U.S. Army Corps of Engineers completed a huge earthen dam, the world's largest at the time, across the Rio Grande just upstream from Cochiti. The dam has forever altered the lives of the pueblo residents and the local environment. The dam and its associated recreational activities bring many visitors to the area, although only a few visit the pueblo. Most visitors come to sail, fish, or swim in Cochiti Lake, the large reservoir created by the dam that backs up water far into White Rock Canyon.

In conjunction with construction of the dam, a residential community for non-Natives, called the Village of Cochiti Lake, was developed on slopes overlooking the lake. The pueblo provided ninety-nine-year leases for home construction and a small commercial center, and formed the Cochiti Community Development Corporation to oversee its operation, a unique situation among the pueblos.

Also in the 1970s, Cochiti became the first pueblo to construct an eighteen-hole golf course. The tribe operates a fine restaurant and pro shop at the links, and also derives income from managing the lake's marina.

In 2001, Tent Rocks National Monument was established to protect a geologically significant formation of tipi-shaped rocks carved into a mountain of volcanic tuff. Ponderosa pine, juniper, and piñon dot the foothills along the cliff face. The area was once part of Cochiti's sphere of influence, but today it falls under the aegis of the Bureau of Land Management. The federal government and Cochiti

Ceremonial drums, Cochiti
Stephen Trimble

tribal authorities will cooperatively manage the monument, and Cochiti will operate a proposed visitor center. The pueblo also hopes to see the land's flora and fauna restored to pre-contact conditions.

Of the pueblo's more than thirteen hundred residents, about twenty families continue to farm and ranch. About eight hundred eighty acres, out of the pueblo's total acreage of nearly fifty-four thousand acres, are devoted to farming, and the pueblo has established the Agricultural Farming Enterprise.

Art, Crafts, and Culture

Cochiti is best known for producing storyteller figures and drums, but the pueblo's artists actually work in a much broader range of media.

Modern storyteller figures were born here in 1964, when Helen Cordero developed this "classic" clay character—typically a grandmotherly woman seated and covered by a swarm of tiny children. Her mouth is open because she is telling a story. The storyteller universe subsequently expanded to include grandfather figures and animals, including bears, turtles, birds, and lizards. Today, storyteller artists work in every pueblo. Another remarkable storyteller artisan is Ada Suina, whose work is displayed prominently at the Albuquerque airport.

But the history of clay figurines at Cochiti goes back much further. In the Spanish era, potters created a style called muños (Spanish for "mimicking doll"), including some based on odd people they met in traveling Mexican circuses. The muños style, mixed with an urban edginess, informs the work of the remarkable contemporary artist Virgil Ortiz, who typically creates black designs on a white base. Virgil also produces precise and creatively designed traditional bowls.

Another of the pueblo's outstanding ceramic artists is Diego Romero, who is producing some of the most novel and important works among the pueblos today. Using clay like a canvas, he paints on designs that have references as diverse as his personal past, pueblo history, and comic books. He also works on paper. His work is displayed at Robert Nichols Gallery, Santa Fe. (505) 747-4827.

COCHITI

Must-see: Tent Rocks, plaza and church, artisans, Cochiti Lake

〰〰〰

July 14: San Buenaventura Feast Day

December 25: buffalo dances

December 26-29: various dances

Other public dances held at various times throughout the year. Call for details.

〰〰〰

P.O. Box 70, Cochiti Pueblo, NM 87072
(505) 465-2244

Drummaking is another traditional skill still practiced by a handful of artisans at Cochiti. In fact, many other pueblos and even Plains tribes get their drums from Cochiti. Among the best drummakers working today are Dave Gordon, Gabe Trujillo, Steve Herrera, and Arnold Herrera.

Steve Herrera has been making fine drums for more than twenty-five years. Drums range in size from less than a foot in diameter to large pow wow styles. He also incorporates drums into nightstands and lamps. Each features a colorful painted acrylic finish.

Cochiti is also home to people working as painters and jewelers. Joe H. Herrera, who won the prestigious Palmes Academiques award from the French government in 1954, was one of the finest Pueblo painters ever. Many Cochiti painters have followed in his footsteps, working in oils, pen and ink, and watercolors. Today, these artists include Bob Chavez, who sells most of his work in Santa Fe. Notable among Cochiti jewelers is award-winning Cippy Crazyhorse, who works in a simple but exquisitely rendered sculptural style of pure silver. He learned the trade from his father, jeweler Joe H. Quintana.

ISLETA

(Iz-LET-tah)

Shiewhibak: "Knife Laid on the Ground to Play Whib"

Drying peaches, Isleta, 1900
SUMNER W. MATTESON

ISLETA MEANS "LITTLE ISLAND" in Spanish, an obvious reference to the pueblo's proximity to the Rio Grande, which once meandered far and wide over a vast flood plain and periodically stranded this pueblo. Today the river is confined, and the pueblo is set on the firm west bank of the Rio Grande.

Historically, Isleta residents derived the majority of their income from farming. The Isleta community controls a large land base of some two hundred eleven thousand acres that extends from the Manzano Mountains in the east across the Rio Grande Valley to the dry mesas of the Rio Puerco in the west. Though close to Albuquerque, Isleta had never been much of a tourist destination before the pueblo developed a major gambling center, golf courses, and other facilities. With a population of more than four thousand residents and more dependable income sources, Isleta looks confidently to the future.

History

Isleta has a unique history among the pueblos. Various villages were established in the area in the 1300s, and in 1675 refugees from the Salinas

left: Corn maiden figurine by Stella Teller, Isleta
STEPHEN TRIMBLE

Pueblos east of the Rio Grande Valley—weary from repeated attacks by Plains Indians—abandoned their villages and settled here. Isleta did not join in the Pueblo Revolt of 1680, and many Isletans accompanied the Spanish when they retreated down the Rio Grande to the El Paso area. Some sources say the Isletans were forced to join the Spanish, who had maintained a presidio at Isleta, while others suggest the people went voluntarily. Whatever the case, in 1692, when the Spanish re-occupied New Mexico, many Isletans chose not to return to their former homes and instead established the village of Ysleta del Sur (Isleta of the South) near El Paso. Today, Ysleta del Sur is one of only two Indian reservations in Texas.

Other Isletans apparently evaded the Spanish and reoccupied their pueblo after the Spanish departed. In December 1681, Spanish Governor Otermin returned on an exploratory mission. He found Isleta inhabited and the church being used as a stock corral. He attacked the pueblo and captured more than five hundred people. The remaining Isletans left the area entirely and settled with the Hopi in Arizona. In the 1700s some returned and reoccupied Isleta. They were joined by Piro refugees from Pilabo Pueblo near Socorro and, later, by people who left Laguna in an internal dispute.

Contemporary Life

The Isleta reservation straddles the Rio Grande, and historically most of its people made a living by farming. It was particularly noted for its vineyards. Today large irrigation ditches still deliver precious water to fields of corn, alfalfa, small orchards, and other crops. Many of the pueblo's men secured off-reservation jobs after World War II, but the development of various reservation business endeavors has enabled more residents to work close to home.

Isleta elects its governor by a general vote of all adults, and is the first pueblo to be served by a female governor.

Art, Crafts, and Culture

Isleta is not known primarily as an artistic center but does have its share of artisans and craftspeople, the majority of whom work in pottery. Isleta potters have developed a distinctive pastel style made by mixing certain slips with a white slip. Celebrated potters include the Ron Martinez, the Chiwiwi family, Augustine Sangre, and storyteller maker Stella Teller.

Noted jewelers Ted Charvez and his daughter Elizabeth Charvez-Caplinger work in precious stones and gold, as do the talented Kirk family members. Also present is the talented painter Ed Shirpoyo, who shows his work at his delightful studio on the main plaza. Handmade fancy dresses for girls and shirts for boys, made by Katherine Williams, are unique to this pueblo. A few artisans weave belts and embroider.

If you've never eaten the crusty and delicious Pueblo-style bread baked in outdoor, beehive-shaped adobe ovens called hornos, or the flat Pueblo fruit pies, head to Isleta, which is home to several bakers.

Isleta is justifiably proud of its whitewashed and twin-towered San Augustine Catholic church,

---

ISLETA

Must-see: San Augustine church, Shirpoyo Art Gallery, a bakery

June: The new governor is honored on the third weekend with various dances

August 28: San Augustine Feast Day with dances in front of the church

September 3-4: evening mass followed by morning procession from the church and afternoon dances in the south plaza

December 24: evening mass and dances in the church

December 25-28: various dances

P.O. Box 1270, Isleta Pueblo, NM 87022
(505) 869-3111
www.indianpueblo.org/isleta

one of New Mexico's more remarkable surviving missions. Originally erected in 1613 and dedicated to San Antonio, it was largely destroyed in the Pueblo Revolt and rebuilt in 1716. Within its massively thick adobe walls you'll find a quiet and lovely refuge. Painted corbels support heavy roof beams, while a hidden clerestory dramatically lights the altar. Unique stained glass windows depict Indian subject matter melded with Christian motifs. Outside, a pretty garden contains a statue of the seventeenth-century Mohawk woman Kateri Tekakwitha, the only American Indian ever to be beatified.

VISITING ISLETA

DIRECTIONS: The village center is located 13 miles south of **Albuquerque**. Head south on I-25 from Albuquerque's Big-I (intersection of I-25 and I-40) for 9.5 miles to Exit 215 and proceed south on NM 47 for 3 miles (passing the **Isleta Gaming Palace**) to NM 147. Turn west (right) and cross the Rio Grande. A dirt road enters the village center, marked by the church bell towers.

VISITOR CENTER/MUSEUM: None.

TOURS: None.

PHOTOGRAPHY: Pictures of the church are allowed without a permit. No photography is allowed of any dance ceremony.

SKETCHING/SOUND RECORDING: Not allowed.

CASINO: **Isleta Gaming Palace**, a 300,000-square-foot, three-story facility, opened in 2001 with table games, slots, restaurants, bar, and gift shop. (505) 877-7ISLETA or www.isletacasinoresort.com.

DINING: The **casino** contains a **sports bar** with light dining options, a buffet restaurant, two snack bars, and a gourmet restaurant with lovely views and table service. For a different lunchtime experience, visit **Katie's Trading Post** (see below), which has a few tables and daily specials, including red-and-green chile, posole, tamales, and Indian tacos, as well as hamburgers and sandwiches.

ACCOMMODATIONS: None available, but Albuquerque has plenty of hotel space.

CAMPING: The **Isleta Lakes Campground** has 40 RV spaces and 100 tent sites located around three lakes near the Rio Grande. Also on site are a laundry, dump station, showers and restrooms, and a convenience store

with propane for sale. The campground is located off NM 47 about one mile south of I-25 at Exit 215. Park your RV (with electric hookups) for $15 per night, or pitch a tent for $12. For details call (505) 877-0370 or write P.O. Box 383, Isleta, NM 87022.

RECREATION: The **Isleta Lakes Recreation Area** is a lovely spot nestled in a cottonwood bosque along the **Rio Grande**. Three manmade ponds shelter turtles and resident and migratory birds, including ducks, coots, swans, and songbirds. If you're lucky, you may spot a squawking great blue heron lifting its great mass off the water. The lakes are stocked with trout, bluegill, and channel catfish. Fishing permits, bait and tackle are available at the convenience store. Permits are $5 for adults, $2.50 for kids under twelve. Picnic and general entry permits are $1 per person over fourteen years old. Wading and swimming are prohibited.

The twenty-seven-hole **Isleta Eagle Golf Course**, set on slightly rolling hills overlooking the Rio Grande Valley, includes a clubhouse, pro shop, and restaurant. It is located directly across NM 47 from the casino. (505) 869-0950.

ARTISTS AND GALLERIES: **Shirpoyo Art Gallery**, one of the nicest galleries to be found at any pueblo, is located near the church on the east side of the main plaza. The gallery is open daily Mar.–Oct., and Nov.–Feb. by appointment. Gregarious artist **Ed Shirpoyo** (Colors in the Sunrise) has a captivating studio and gallery that features realistic scenes of Pueblo life in acrylics, oils, watercolor, and pen and ink. He also offers a selection of turn-of-the-century pottery by Hopi and other Pueblo artists, jewelry by Navajo and Pueblo artisans, and Arizona baskets. The gallery, which **Shirpoyo** has run for more than three decades, is located in his family's

historic residence. (505) 869-0049.

Katie's Trading Post is a charming, converted 1930s-era gas station that offers a bit of everything. A selection of jewelry by Navajo, Santo Domingo, and Isleta artisans; handmade and cast pottery including works by Isleta artist **Augustine Sangre**; and traditional Pueblo-style shawls and mantas made by owner **Katherine Williams**. Also look for handmade girls' dresses and boys' shirts, Pendleton blankets, beaded goods from South Dakota, commercial Navajo sandpaintings, and a wide variety of foods, including hot meals, horno-baked bread, Pueblo-style flat pie, and blue cornmeal mixes. There are a few small tables for dining. Located at the intersection of NM 314 and NM 45, on the far west side of the reservation, (505) 869-6316. Closed Sun.–Mon.

Hummingbird offers a selection of poured ceramic and traditional pottery, portraits and pottery paintings by Navajo artist **Cleveland**, woven bags and jewelry, and snacks. Located two blocks east of the main plaza. Open daily. The shop accepts cash and checks only.

The **Kirk** family—including **Michael**, **Melanie**, and **Andy**—are master jewelers who set a wide variety of precious and semiprecious stones in gold and other materials. www.indianvillage.com. **Michael:** (505) 869-3317 or MKJewelry@aol.com. **Melanie:** (505) 869-3638 or KirkLente@aol.com. **Andy:** (505) 869-6098 or AndysallyK@aol.com.

Ron "Looking Elk" Martinez, of Isleta/Taos heritage, produces a fine range of pottery, including vessels featuring stone-polished red- and black-ware, and a beautiful, deep brown finish created from the smoke of cottonwood bark. The tribal member's bowls, vases, and wedding vases are often etched. 330 Tribal Rd., #65, Albuquerque, MN 87105, (505) 869-5254.

JEMEZ

(HEY-mez)

He-mish: "The People"

Jemez is the sole remaining pueblo out of six sites that once dotted the rugged southern end of the Jemez Mountains, and some of its residents are descendants of the people of Pecos Pueblo. Set in the deep, dramatic, red-walled Cañon de San Diego alongside the Jemez River, the pueblo has an active arts community particularly noted for a wide variety of pottery styles. Jemez's historic main village is closed to the public, except on a handful of days, so artists and craftspeople operate small studios and galleries on or near the state highway. Travelers are also encouraged to stop at the new Walatowa Visitor Center on NM 4.

Harvesting corn, Jemez, 1936

T. HARMON PARKHURST

VISITING JEMEZ

DIRECTIONS: Located 55 miles northwest of **Albuquerque** on the **Jemez Mountain National Scenic Byway**. From Albuquerque or Santa Fe, take I-25 to **Bernalillo** and Exit 242. Head west 23 miles on NM 44/US 550 to the village of **San Ysidro**. Turn north (right) onto NM 4 and proceed 6 miles to the **Walatowa Visitor Center**, passing through historic Jemez village center en route.

VISITOR CENTER/MUSEUM: The **Walatowa Visitor Center** houses a 1200-square-foot museum hall including historic photos, prehistoric Jemez black-and-white pottery, other Jemez and Spanish artifacts, a replica of a traditional field house, and examples of contemporary Jemez art, including pottery. It also offers a gift shop, conference facilities, and restrooms. The facility also doubles as an orientation center for the nearby national forest. The visitor center is located a few miles north of the historic village on NM 4 at Red Rocks. Open daily, fall–spring 10 A.M.–4 P.M., summer 8 A.M.–5 P.M.

TOURS: Options include guided tours of artist studios and lunch with the artists; bread-baking, pottery-firing and other arts demonstrations; dancing; and storytelling. Another tour explores natural wonders and historic sites of the region, including **Jemez State Monument**, **Soda Dam**, **Valle Grande**, and **Bandelier National Monument**. Also offered are a half-day guided fishing outing with a sack lunch, or an all-day experience with a lakeside evening cookout. A minimum of sixteen people is required for the tours, with fees ranging from $25 to $40 per person. Reservations are required.

PHOTOGRAPHY: Not allowed within the traditional pueblo village, but permitted at **Jemez Red Rocks Area**. Commercial photography requires a permit.

SKETCHING/SOUND RECORDING: Not allowed.

DINING: Group meals may be arranged with advance notice through the **Walatowa Visitor Center** or a few pueblo residents (see below). During major public events, and on most weekends from April through October, **roadside vendors** sell tasty New Mexican and Pueblo-style foods at **Red Rocks**. The town of **Jemez Springs**, 12 miles north of the pueblo on NM 4, offers a handful of restaurants, including the historic **Los Ojos**.

ACCOMMODATIONS: Several options exist in the nearby town of **Jemez Springs**.

RECREATION: Jemez offers **fishing** for rainbow trout, channel catfish, and largemouth bass at its **Holy Ghost** and **Dragonfly Lakes** from Apr. 1–Oct. 30, sunrise to sunset. The lakes are located off NM 44, twenty-three miles northwest of **San Ysidro**. Day permits cost $8 for adults and $6 for children under fourteen and seniors. There is an eight-fish limit. Picnicking is allowed, but there are no shelters. Call (505) 834-7533.

ARTISTS AND GALLERIES: A comprehensive list of more than forty artists, many with contact information and photographs of work posted, can be found on the **pueblo's web site**. Works can be purchased on-line with MasterCard, Visa, or American Express.

A handful of studio and galleries are operated in **Jemez village** itself. All are either right on, or just off, NM 4. **Storytellers by Fragua** represents the work of **Rose Fragua** and other family members. There you will discover a variety of storytellers, koshare (clowns), turtle, and frog figurines, corn maidens, friendship bowls, and other works. Located at 109 Big Bear, west of NM 4 at mile marker five. (505) 834-9308. Open daily.

The **Toyas** offer a selection of storytellers, wedding vases, friendship bowls, Nativity sets, and Christmas ornaments made by **Persingula Toya**. You also will find melon bowls and jewelry. The family occasionally opens a food booth, serving traditional frybread, chile, and beans, and can prepare group dinners with advance notice. Located at 4524 NM 4, across the road from the Tribal Administration Building. (505) 834-7347. Open daily but call first. Credit cards accepted.

Other commercial galleries include the **Yepa** family's **Sun-n-Fire Pottery** (4514 NM 4); **Dancing Corn Gallery**, featuring the pottery of **Marie Romero** and family (4025 NM 4, on the south edge of the village); and **Jemez Silverwork** (27 Antelope Hill Rd. off Buffalo Hill Road east of NM 4).

Ruby Panana was raised at Zia but resides at Jemez. The fourth-generation potter, who has won many awards, often incorporates the typical Zia big-eyed, split-tailed birds in her work. P.O. Box 426, Jemez Pueblo, NM, 87024, (505) 834-7629.

In addition to storytellers, **Lorraine Chinana** also produces handsome pottery with a gray surface that she carves to reveal an underlying tan subsurface. P.O. Box 413, Jemez Pueblo, NM 87024, (505) 834-7463.

Jemez sculptor **Cliff Fragua** received a commission in 2000 from the state of New Mexico to create a statue of Pueblo Revolt leader Popé, which will be displayed in **Statuary Hall** in the **U.S. Capitol** in **Washington**, D.C. (505) 892-6516 or singingstudio.com.

Joe V. Cajero has carved out a popular niche for himself with his often humorous and finely detailed clay and bronze renderings of Pueblo koshares. P.O. Box 377, Jemez Pueblo, NM 87024, (505) 867-3773, www.rt66.com/~jacajero.

Potters represented at the **Walatowa Visitor Center** include **Michelle Mora** (redware with black and tan geometric designs and melon bowls), **Mary Helen Loretto** (stone-polished seed pots painted with katsina faces, feathers, and geometric designs in black, red, and tan), **Gabriel Cajero** (large, carved vases), and **Anita Cajero** (friendship pots, stepped-edged kiva pots, and storytellers). Other potters represented include **Amelia Galvan**, **Juana Chinana**, **Shirley Chinana**, and **Helen Shendo**.

Also on view are a larger-than-life-sized female dancer carved from Colorado marble by **Clifford Fragua**, a wide selection of jewelry (including bead necklaces, rings, and earrings), hand-carved flutes by **Robert Mirabal** of Taos Pueblo, large handmade drums by **Patrick Romero**, and traditional woven belts and sashes of black, red, white, and green yarn.

The shop also sells books on Southwestern and Native American subjects. The latter include works by Jemez historian **Joe Sando** and Kiowa author **N. Scott Momaday**, whose Pulitzer Prize-winning novel, *House Made of Dawn*, is set in Jemez Pueblo.

History

Immigrants from the Four Corners region first established permanent settlements in the Jemez area between 1275 and 1350. When the Spanish first entered the Jemez area in 1541, they found about half a dozen large, masonry pueblos firmly rooted in the rough but beautiful canyons and mesas at the southern end of the Jemez Mountains. Among these early pueblos were Kwastiyukwa (Place of Pine Birds) and Gytotahownlanew (Place Where the Giant Stepped), both as tall as five stories in some portions and containing more than three thousand rooms. Another was named Sayshukwa (Eagle Dwelling Place), which was occupied from 1350 to 1700. These pueblos and hundreds of smaller living units used in summer as base camps for hunting, gathering, and agricultural activities are believed to have sheltered as many as thirty thousand persons in the sixteenth century. But the people succumbed to superior Spanish weapons and Spanish-introduced diseases to which they had no immunity, and by the eighteenth century the Jemez population had fallen to as few as three hundred survivors living in the current village.

This village, named Walatowa (The Place), was founded about 1400 as a trade center. It was abandoned in 1680, and reoccupied between 1703 and 1720. By 1838, disease, raids by nomadic Indian tribes, and other factors had reduced mighty Pecos Pueblo to about seventeen persons. That year the surviving inhabitants of Pecos abandoned their homelands and moved to Jemez, whose residents also spoke Towa. Jemez Pueblo celebrates this legacy with the Pecos bull dance, presented every August 1.

The Jemez people once farmed on a large scale. Up to the 1900s, more than two thousand

Storyteller doll sculptor Juanita Fragua's workbench, Jemez
STEPHEN TRIMBLE

acres were usually under cultivation. The primary crops were wheat (introduced by Franciscan friars), corn, and chile, as well as lesser amounts of squash, cotton, tobacco, grapes, and fruits, including peaches, apricots, plums, and cherries.

Contemporary Life

Today, about thirty four hundred tribal members of Jemez Pueblo engage in a limited amount of farming and livestock production. Most adults commute to Albuquerque, while one hundred sixty or so work for the tribe. In 2000, the pueblo administration launched a new tribal endeavor, Walatowa

Woodlands, which produces custom-cut vigas for homebuilding and rough-hewn lumber for furniture. The wood is harvested from forest-thinning operations on tribal lands.

The Jemez reservation covers ninety thousand acres, but does not include the prehistoric pueblo sites, which are located on national forest lands.

Art, Crafts, and Culture

Traditionally, Jemez artisans produced a fine pottery with an oyster-white base and black geometric designs above, as well as several cruder styles. But pottery production ceased in the mid-eighteenth century, and Jemez came to rely on decorated pottery obtained through trade with their Keresan neighbors, primarily Zia. Around 1900, Jemez residents resumed making pottery on a limited scale, and today's potters have elevated the craft to a fine art.

Jemez potters are perhaps best known for their black-on-red and black/red-on-tan work. But artists are also producing highly polished, elaborately engraved redware (called *sgraffito*), and have adopted many other pueblos' styles and forms, as well. Jemez artists such as Esther Cajero, Lavern Loretto-Tosa, Lorraine Chinana, Anita Cajero, and Carol G. Lucero Gachupin create a wide variety of story-tellers, including female and male figures, and figures with shawls and in moccasins. Other artists produce swirl melon bowls, wedding vases, friendship pots (pinch pots with figures of children around the lip), a charming variety of holiday ornaments, Nativity sets, and seed bowls. Other artists, including Shadrack Tosa and Martha Toya, create clay animal figurines. Several artists produce clay "corn maidens" emerging from ears of corn. Juanita Fragua makes cream-colored works painted with brown and black corn stalks or geometric patterns, and shiny cream-colored pieces embellished with tiny hand imprints.

Artists also work in jewelry, embroidery and belt weaving, and sculpture. These include Cliff Fragua, whose works are found in major Southwestern collections; Matthew Panana, who has been sculpting for fifteen years; James Vigil, who puts an unmistakable twist on character studies; and Joe Cajero. Jemez is also home to the notable painter Felix Vigil, and traditional drummaker Patrick Romero. Romero learned his trade from his father Santiago, who sold aspen log drums in the 1940s at the Santa Fe Railway station in Albuquerque.

The village church, San Diego de Jemez Mission, was built around 1880 and extensively remodeled in the early 1990s.

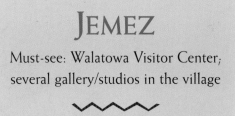

JEMEZ

Must-see: Walatowa Visitor Center; several gallery/studios in the village

Ceremonial dances are held throughout the year in historic Jemez village, and a handful of events are open to visitors.

The Walatowa Visitor Center hosts arts-and-crafts demonstrations, exhibition dances, bread-baking in traditional hornos, and other events during summer weekends. The Towa Arts and Crafts Committee organizes the annual Memorial Weekend Jemez Red Rocks Arts and Crafts Show, and the Winter Arts and Crafts Show (held on the first weekend in December at the Jemez Civic Center on NM 4 in Cañones between the historic village and the Walatowa Visitor Center).

P.O. Box 100, Jemez Pueblo, NM 87024
(505) 834-7235
www.jemezpueblo.org.

This is one of the most comprehensive and informative Pueblo tribal web sites available, with sections on and links to Jemez artists, tour information, details on the Walatowa Visitor Center, a pueblo overview, and more.

LAGUNA

(lah-GOO-nah)

Ka-waikah: "Lake People"

San Jose de Laguna Mission and pueblo, Laguna
MARK NOHL

LAGUNA HAS ONE OF THE LARGEST LAND reserves of all the pueblos, and is the youngest, having been founded in 1699. Most visitors see only a fraction of its terrain as they zoom along busy I-40, perhaps noting the ancient-looking adobe village of Old Laguna capped by the white San Jose Mission.

If you choose to stop, exit onto a stretch of fabled Route 66, the nation's first transcontinental roadway, which rolls along Old Laguna village's northern edge.

Farther off the highway are a handful of other, more remote Laguna villages nestled in broad canyons beneath huge mesas that back up to towering Mount Taylor, which reaches an elevation of 11,301 feet. The canyons snake out of the mesas, offering beautiful views to the south across the Rio San Jose Valley and to the distant Rio Grande Valley in the east.

The main village, Old Laguna, and the smaller villages of Paraje, Paguate, Mesita, Encinal, and Seama are home to a number of artists and craftspeople. At Old Laguna you'll find a handful of small arts-and-crafts shops and places to buy horno-baked bread, and a gas station with a grocery and a deli.

Guests are welcome during the pueblo's two main feast days in Old Laguna, as well as at various ceremonies and dances held at the outlying villages.

History

Laguna was officially established in 1699 under the direction of Spanish Governor Cubero by groups of Pueblo people from the immediate area, as well as by other Keres-speaking refugees of the Rio Grande Valley, including Cochiti and Santo Domingo pueblos that were hard hit during the re-conquest by Spanish Governor Diego de Vargas.

Oral history and archeology reveal that the area in and around Laguna was occupied off and on for thousands of years by various Indian peoples. The Laguna people say that one of their leaders,

Drying chilies, Laguna
STEPHEN TRIMBLE

Broken Prayer Stick, once led a group of people from a place called Shipop to a spot where beavers had created a laguna by damming a small river. The people settled here and eventually established a village they named Ka-waikah. The exact site of this village is uncertain, but most likely lies under Old Laguna.

In the 1700s, the fertile Rio San Jose Valley began to attract non-Indian settlers. This continued in the early American era of the mid-nineteenth century and competition over resources and land increased. In 1851 a Protestant missionary, the Reverend Samuel Gorman, took up residence at the pueblo, and other Anglo-Americans soon joined him. In the 1870s, the pueblo split into factions of religious traditionalists and Protestant adherents. As a result, two kivas were destroyed and the conservative faction moved permanently to Isleta Pueblo.

In the 1880s, the Santa Fe Railway extended its tracks across the reservation, following the natural east-west travel corridor along the Rio San Jose. This brought further changes to the previously isolated reservation. Pueblo artists and craftsmen were able to sell their goods directly to tourist train passengers during brief rest stops. Many Laguna men also found employment with the Santa Fe Railway, laying track, maintaining locomotives

and rolling stock, and serving in other roles. A substantial number of these rail workers and their families relocated to towns farther down the line, in Arizona and California, where many of their descendants remain today. Some sent money home when they could, and eventually returned to the reservation.

In 1926, U.S. Route 66 reached the Rio San Jose Valley, snaking through several Laguna villages and introducing a new generation of tourists to Pueblo culture.

Contemporary Life

Capitalizing on Laguna's importance as a travel corridor, in 1999 the pueblo opened a small casino on I-40, which should generate much-needed income for tribal infrastructure, social services, and educational programs. Adjoining the casino is the tribally owned Dancing Eagle Market with a handful of tribal and non-tribal business tenants. The tribe also runs a large construction business that specializes in mine reclamation and nuclear clean-up operations. Many of the tribe's seventy-six hundred enrolled members live and work in Albuquerque. Fewer than half of Laguna's enrolled tribal members live and work on the reservation.

Laguna's 425,000-acre reservation is blessed with a substantial natural resource base. The world's largest open-pit uranium mine operated here for several decades, but is now closed and the land reclaimed. The tribe grazes cattle, sheep, and horses on its extensive grasslands, and permits public hunting for elk and other big game that roam the valley floors, canyon rims, mesas, and slopes of Mount Taylor.

Art, Crafts, and Culture

Laguna has a fair number of artists and craftspeople, even though it is not considered a major locale for arts nor a tourist center. Its artisans are most active in pottery. Gladys Paquin often works in polychrome designs of naturalistic (such as animals and cloud forms) and geometric elements over a white base. Evelyn Cheromiah, her daughters Lee Ann and Mary, and her grandson Brooke are accomplished traditional potters. Cheromiah often works with

VISITING LAGUNA

DIRECTIONS: Located 46 miles west of **Albuquerque** on I-40. Take Exit 114 and proceed 1 mile west on NM 124 (old U.S. Route 66) to reach Old Laguna. The Governor's Office is on Capital Drive. **San Jose Mission** is up the hill.

There are five other villages on the reservation. **Paraje** is a few miles west of **Old Laguna** just off NM 124. **Paguate** and **Seama** are 9 and 13 miles away, respectively, on NM 279. **Encinal** is 5 miles west of **Old Laguna** on Tribal Road 49, off NM 24. **Mesita** is located east of **Old Laguna** on NM 124. **La Questa Overlook** is on a side road to NM 279, 1? miles off NM 124.

TOURS: Tours conducted by **Ann Rose Ray** are offered year round, and can be customized for feast day outings, artist studios, photo tours, history, daily life, school and groups. She can also arrange traditional meals. P.O. Box 184, Laguna, NM 87026. (505) 552-9771 or annrose99@hotmail.com. She prefers two weeks' advance notice.

PHOTOGRAPHY: A free permit (available at the Governor's Office) is required, but photography of ceremonies in all villages is prohibited.

SKETCHING/SOUND RECORDING: Not allowed.

CASINO: The **Dancing Eagle Casino** offers slots, craps, roulette, and blackjack. Located off I-40 at Exit 108. (877) 440-9969 or (505) 552-1111.

DINING: The **Dancing Eagle Casino** has a good restaurant that features daily lunch and dinner specialties, pasta, and gourmet pizza; and a snack bar. **Grandma Jo's Bakery** in the **Dancing Eagle Market** produces tasty breads (both traditional style and wheat), and pies (both Pueblo flat style and regular). On Tuesdays, drop in for Navajo tacos and frybread.

ACCOMMODATIONS: Nearby is the luxurious **Apache Canyon Ranch Bed and Breakfast**, which has four luxury rooms (including the **Laguna** and **Sky City** rooms with fireplaces and private whirlpool tubs) and a 750-square-foot guesthouse, guided horseback riding, and massage by a Jemez Pueblo

masseuse. Located on the **To' Hajiilee Navajo** reservation east of Laguna. (505) 836-7220.

RECREATION: The tribe conducts guided **bow** and **rifle hunts** on the reservation. Contact the Governor's Office.

ARTISTS AND GALLERIES: Laguna artists and craftspeople sell handmade goods, especially pottery and jewelry, and food from booths located at rest areas along I-40 near **Old Laguna**. Several shops in various Laguna villages are also open to the public.

The **Indian Art Center** presents a range of arts and crafts from Laguna and other pueblos. The largest body of work is pottery from artists such as **Lee Ann Cheromiah**, but the center also features horsehair pottery and "traditional" pitch-polished Navajo pottery. Jewelry includes copper bracelets by **Greg Lewis**, and work by Zuni, Navajo, and Hopi artisans. There also is a nice selection of katsinas and rattles by **Ted Francis** and apparel by **Denise Kirksey**. Located in Old Laguna on NM 214, one-half mile off I-40 at Exit 114. (505) 552-0048. Open daily in summer, including major holidays, otherwise Mon.–Sat. Credit cards accepted.

Photographer **Lee Marmon** has been documenting Pueblo life for more than thirty-five years. He welcomes serious visitors to his studio home. Located behind the Old Laguna post office. (505) 552-6451. Open year round but call first.

Turquoise Maiden features apparel, including velvet dresses and blouses with silver buttons, made by **Denise Kirksey**. Located in New Laguna. (505) 552-7141. By appointment only.

San Jose Gift Shop carries Laguna pottery, crosses and jewelry in turquoise and silver, and statues of Catholic saints. The shop adjoins the Old Laguna church. (505) 552-0031. Open daily late spring through mid fall, 9 A.M.–3 P.M., otherwise by appointment.

Herrera Pottery features the traditional pottery of **Ruth Koyona** and the ceramic pottery of her daughter **Sherril Pedro**. **Julia P. Herrera** also displays jewelry by **Yvonne Lewis** of Laguna/Cochiti heritage, jewelry from Zuni and Santo Domingo, and unique Navajo cloth storyteller dolls. Located

next to San Jose Mission. (505) 552-6148. Open daily 9 A.M.–6 P.M.

Naiya Gifts features the handmade, carved pottery of owner **Rita Suazo** (Hopi), her husband **Dale Suazo** (Taos), and **Mike Kanteena** (Laguna). The shop also carries manufactured pottery with hand painted glazes, including "food safe" mugs, bowls, and cups. She also stocks Laguna, Hopi, and Zuni jewelry, shawls and baby blankets, pillows, painted wooden wall plaques, and even a painted leather cell phone holder. Located in **Paraje**, west of Old Laguna, just off NM 124. (505) 552-7693 or rsuazo@7cities.net. Open Mon.–Fri. 10 A.M.–6 P.M., Sat.–Sun. 11 A.M.–3 P.M.

Sweetie's is a flower shop and arts-and-crafts gallery located in a former gas station. Goods found here include small, colorful yucca baskets woven by **Marvin Fernando**. Owner **Jeanette Sarracino** provides her own traditional pottery. There's also acrylic-painted pottery and storytellers from Jemez, animal figurines, and ceramic Christmas ornaments, sugar bowls, salt and pepper shakers. A selection of girl's traditional ceremonial clothing, including aprons, dresses, and scarves, as well as crocheted blankets, is also available. Located on NM 124 in the village of **New Laguna**, 3 miles west of Old Laguna. (505) 552-6361, (877) 552-6361, or www.sweeties-in-laguna.com. Open summer weekdays 9 A.M.–6 P.M., otherwise weekdays 10 A.M.–5 P.M. Major charge cards accepted.

Ken Romero, of Taos and Laguna descent, produces jewelry featuring fine assemblies of cut and polished stones set in gold. (505) 836-3103 or www.ncaied.org/kromero

Potter **Michael Kanteena** specializes in both contemporary and unique prehistoric "recreations," often a simple black on beige. P.O. Box 77, New Laguna, NM 87038. (505) 552-6710, www.photojan.com.

The **Dancing Eagle Supermarket** has a fine selection of Pueblo arts and crafts, including Laguna and Acoma pottery; Zuni and Navajo jewelry; beadwork; and contemporary carved wood snakes. Miniature katsina dolls carved by **Mike Henshaw** are especially popular. From I-40, take Exit 108. Open daily 7 A.M.–9 P.M., including major holidays. Credit cards accepted.

geometric designs in vessels ranging from small bowls to large vases. A handful of artisans also work as jewelers. In addition, a few folks carve in wood, paint, weave belts and kilts, and make moccasins.

LAGUNA

Must-see: San Jose Mission church at Old Laguna, St. Margaret Mary at Paraje, views from La Questa Overlook, shops and artist studios

January 6: King's Day
with dances at Old Laguna

March 19: San Jose Feast Day with harvest and other dances at Old Laguna

July 26: St. Anne Feast Day
with harvest and other dances at Mesita

September (TBA): annual All-Indian Baseball Tournament

September 8: Santa Maria Feast Day at Encinal

September 19: San Jose Harvest Feast Day at Old Laguna

September 25: Saint Elizabeth Feast Day at Paguate

October 17: Saint Margaret Mary Feast Day at Paraje

December 24: Christmas mass at 10 P.M. followed by harvest, arrow, deer, and other dances at San Jose church, Old Laguna

December 25-28: dances at all the villages

Address: Attention Victor Sarracino, P.O. Box 194, Laguna Pueblo, NM 87026 Governor's Office, (505) 552-6654, ext. 1200

Denise Kirksey produces beautiful velvet clothing, and Marvin Fernando is one of the few artisans among any of the pueblos producing baskets.

Laguna is home to Lee Marmon, one of New Mexico's outstanding photographers. Marmon's work has been featured in books, on posters, and in many magazines. Sixteen of his photomurals hang in the Denver Airport. They reveal the photographer's keen eye for detail and composition and portray rarely seen, and sometimes humorous, aspects of Pueblo life. He welcomes visitors. His daughter, well-known writer Leslie Marmon Silko, spent her formative years at Laguna. Her novels, *Gardens in the Dunes* and *Ceremony;* her autobiography, *Sacred Water;* her book of poetry, *Laguna Woman*, and other works reflect a distinctive Pueblo sensibility.

At the center of the village of Old Laguna is San Jose Mission church, which looks as if it could take flight like a white dove over the Rio San Jose Valley. Erected in 1699, it is one of the nation's oldest Catholic churches. (The 1811 date, carved into a beam in the choir loft, refers to the completion of a restoration project.) Built after the Pueblo Revolt, San Jose was never burned or looted and looks essentially the same today as when it was first erected. Its distinctive and often-photographed twin-bell belfry makes this a true New Mexico landmark.

Inside, on its cool, thick walls of stone, adobe and plaster, between the packed mud floors and the Stations of the Cross, are a series of painted, linked geometric designs—swirls, steps, triangles, arches, and an occasional bird. The captivating altar screen consists of four painted images of saints and six red-and-green spiral posts carved by an unknown Laguna santero. The foot of the altar area is decorated in typical Pueblo cloth of white cotton with red, green, and black designs, while the ceiling is painted with images of a rainbow flanked by the sun and moon. Supporting the altar railing are carved and painted katsinas. On the ceiling, latillas are alternately painted yellow, black, and red. Pottery candleholders round out the distinctive setting. (505) 552-9330. Open year round, Mon.–Fri. 9 A.M.–3 P.M., Sunday services at 10 A.M.

NAMBE

(Nahm-BAY)

Nambe: "Place of Bowl-Shaped Earth"

NAMBE IS NOT ON THE COMMON tourist trail, despite the fact that it is among the closest to Santa Fe. The pueblo is blessed with a dramatic location in the beautiful foothills of the Sangre de Cristo Mountains, and natural wonders dot the reservation. Towering above the pueblo is a heavily forested mountain range capped by Santa Fe Baldy.

From the often-snow-capped summits run numerous creeks and streams, including the Rio Nambe, which has cut a canyon several hundred feet deep as it flows through the reservation. A dam in this canyon has formed a sizeable lake where you can fish, and below the dam you can hike to some impressive waterfalls. Elsewhere stand odd and impressive monumental earthen formations, like modern art in an ancient land.

Nambe has undergone a cultural revitalization the past few decades. New artists emerging here are producing distinctive work, and there is a greater emphasis on the pueblo's traditional ceremonies.

Kiva and Sangre de Cristo range, Nambe, 1940
FERENZ FEDOR

Visiting Nambe

DIRECTIONS: Located 20 miles northwest of **Santa Fe**. From US 84/285, turn east (right) onto NM 503 and proceed 3 miles to the pueblo entry road marked "**Nambe Falls**." Turn east (right), proceed 1.5 miles, and then turn right onto an unpaved road to reach the Governor's Office and main plaza. The lake and falls are located several miles farther up the main road.

VISITOR CENTER/MUSEUM: A few historic artifacts unearthed in an archeological dig conducted by Southern Methodist University are displayed at the **Governor's Office**. Open weekdays 8 A.M.–5 P.M.

TOURS: Tours to view the tribe's **buffalo herd** can be arranged through the Governor's Office, or you may visit the herd on your own during daylight hours. To get there, drive 1 mile down the dirt road directly across from the entrance road to the Governor's Office. The herd often gathers around a water tank behind a tall fence. **Cloud Eagle** can also arrange tours with advance notice. (Contact information appears below.)

VISITING INFORMATION: Large groups visiting the reservation should contact the Governor's Office in advance.

PHOTOGRAPHY: Still photo permits (for personal, noncommercial use only) run $10 a day, and are available at the Governor's Office. Video permits are also available. Photography of ceremonies is not allowed.

SKETCHING/SOUND RECORDING: Sketching permits are available through the Governor's Office. Sketching of ceremonies is not allowed.

DINING: Many options are close by in **Santa Fe** and **Española**.

ACCOMMODATIONS: Many choices exist in **Santa Fe** and **Española**.

CAMPING: There is a nice campground with 12 RV sites (with electricity and water hookups) and tent sites located at the foot of the **Nambe Falls Canyon**. Large cottonwood trees and ramadas provide ample shade. Camping fees are $20 per night or $30 with hookups. The campground is generally open March through late September, depending on weather. There are also camping sites in nearby **Santa Fe National Forest**.

RECREATION: **Lake Nambe**, a reservoir created by an impressive dam rising 150 feet from the streambed, is located a few miles east of the village center. The access road provides breathtaking views westward across the **Rio Grande Valley**.

The lake is stocked with **rainbow trout** that average 14 inches, although many have been caught in the 18- to 22-inch range and a 27-inch record-breaker was caught in 2000. Fishing permits cost $10 per day for adults, $6 for seniors and kids under twelve. The catch limit is seven fish a day. Boats may be used on the lake, but only electric motors are permitted. A state fishing license is not required. Swimming in the lake is not allowed.

The lake is usually open daily from sunrise to sunset from March until the end of September, weather permitting. Visitors may reserve picnic shelters with shade, fire pits and tables for $20. Fishing supplies and snacks are available at the ranger station. Stream fishing is prohibited.

Below the dam and lake, a narrow, deep canyon snakes down toward the pueblo. Nestled in the canyon are a couple of lovely **waterfalls** with deep pools. The banks of the perennial stream are dotted with a colorful mixture of oak, willow, mountain cottonwood, juniper, chamisa, and wildflowers. The canyon trailhead is located at the **Nambe Falls Recreation Area**, and the hike to the falls takes about twenty minutes at a moderate pace. Hikers must scramble over a few boulders and, in wet years, wade across the stream.

The recreation area offers covered ramadas and other shelters with tables and fire pits. Portable toilets are available. A $5 picnic fee is payable at the recreation area fee station. To get to the recreation area and trail to the falls, turn right at the ranger station onto a good gravel road and follow it to the canyon mouth.

ARTISTS AND GALLERIES: No formal art galleries exist here, but several artists run small shops out of their homes, and others encourage visits from serious potential buyers. For a detailed list and map, contact the Governor's Office.

Michael "NaNa Ping" Garcia, of Pascua Yaqui heritage, whose wife is from Nambe, is a popular jeweler who works predominantly in fine inlay work with a wide array of colorful stones set in gold and silver. (505) 455-2093, NaNa Ping@aol.com, www.hometown.aol.com/nanping.

Potter **Pearl Talachy** creates simply formed, lightly carved vessels in lovely deep brown and black tones. Rt. 1, Box 114M, Nambe Pueblo, NM 87501. (505) 455-3429.

Sculptor, painter, and graphic artist **Cloud Eagle** is also a noted teacher who conducts Indian youth after-school and apprentice programs at his studio. He can also arrange dance presentations, traditional foods and meals, storytelling, talks, art demonstrations, tours, and other services for groups with advance notice. (505) 455-2662. Studio is open summer weekdays but call first. Major credit cards are accepted.

Other Nambe artists include **Shannon McKenna** (silver jewelry, moccasins, drums, beadwork), **Doreen Mirabal** (pottery, manta weaving), and **Tony Perez** (pottery animal figurines). Also look for works by **Cami Porter** (painting, beading), **Nathaniel Porter** (gourd painting, beading), **Sue Sanchez** (woven belts), and **Wanda Tafoya** (pottery). Collectors also should see works by **Carlos Vigil** (painting), **Gordon Vigil** (sculpture), **Lonnie Vigil** (extraordinary micaceous vessels), **Benjamin Yates** (beadwork, bow and flint-arrow making, hide tanning, moccasins, rattles, drums), and **Herbert Yates** (pottery, headdresses).

History

Nambe's roots extend into prehistory. It once served as a cultural and religious center for the Tewa-speaking Pueblo peoples. Nambe people participated in the Pueblo Revolt of 1680. Following the Spanish reoccupation of the region in the 1700s, Hispanic settlers usurped much of the pueblo's historic land base.

Contemporary Life

Nambe's isolated locale has kept it out of the mainstream, and it displays a look and ambiance that has remained largely unchanged for decades. However, in 1974 the U.S. Bureau of Reclamation built a major dam on the Rio Nambe that flooded much of the pueblo's prehistoric residence sites but created a lake that the tribe today manages as an income source. The pueblo also has begun to encourage tourism. The pueblo has about six hundred enrolled members, and most adults are employed in Santa Fe or at Los Alamos National Laboratories. The tribe also maintains about two dozen buffalo for spiritual reasons and is encouraging organic farming.

Along US 84/285, on a portion of the tribe's 19,000-acre land base, the tribe is developing several business ventures, including a 150-acre industrial park, a mobile home park, and a recycling facility.

Art, Crafts, and Culture

The pueblo is home to several dozen artists. Perhaps the best known is Lonnie Vigil, who produces lovely micaceous pottery enhanced with black and gray "cloud" patterns left by smoke from the firing process. Other potters work in black-on-black pottery, a white-on-red style, redware, and matte-and-polished polychrome. Painted designs of katsina faces, plumed water serpents, paw prints, feathers, and animals appear in black, reddish orange, bluish gray, and white.

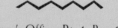
Another well-known and respected artist, Cloud Eagle, works as a contemporary and traditional sculptor in stone, wood, ceramic, and metal arts. He also produces paintings and graphic arts. Other residents weave traditional cotton belts and kilts and work as painters, jewelers, beaders, moccasin cobblers, drummakers, and sculptors.

Most traditional dances are held in the village plaza, located within sight of the Governor's Office. The plaza features an ancient round kiva with straw-flecked adobe walls and well-worn, radiating wooden steps. Also facing the plaza is San Francisco church, built about 1974.

PICURIS

(pee-kuhr-EES)

Pikuri: "Those Who Paint"

PICURIS IS THE MOUNTAIN PUEBLO. The small village is tucked into a beautiful high valley that winds westward out of the sawtoothed Truchas Peaks of the Sangre de Cristo Mountains. Alongside the beautiful Rio Pueblo, lush meadows bordered by deciduous trees rise up to pine-covered slopes of the Picuris Range, which borders the village to the north. Elk and deer graze in the meadows, trout dart in the cold clear streams, and red-tailed hawks patrol the skies.

The village's isolated aerie guards some impressive ruins, including a rare tower kiva, from its days when the pueblo was a mighty power. The pueblo also is home to a remarkable Catholic church, and despite the community's relatively small population it also has one of the nicer pueblo visitor centers and tribal museums.

History

The Picuris people believe their ancestors first settled in their "hidden valley" as early as A.D. 1150. More residents joined them about 1250, after abandoning a nearby village archeologists

Firing pots by Cora and Anthony Duran, Picuris

STEPHEN TRIMBLE

call Pot Creek, which had a prehistoric population of about three thousand. (The site is located at Ft. Burgwin Research Center, just off NM 518.) Over the next three centuries, the people of Picuris constructed a pueblo seven or eight stories high, making it the tallest of all the prehistoric pueblos and perhaps the largest, as well.

Much of the pueblo's prosperity was a consequence of geography. Like Taos, its Tiwa-speaking neighbor to the north, Picuris lies close to two major passes through the Sangre de Cristo Mountains to the Great Plains beyond. Nomadic tribes, including Apache bands, often came to Picuris to trade. They would camp outside the pueblo in temporary shelters and barter buffalo hides, game pelts, robes, tallow, and jerky for Picuris corn, pottery, turquoise, and textiles.

The Coronado expedition of 1540 missed Picuris, and the Spanish did not encounter the town until Castaño de Sosa first approached it through deep snow in January 1591.

Like other Tiwa-speaking peoples of the area, the Picuris people participated in the Pueblo Revolt of 1680, and paid for it. Don Diego de Vargas led a punitive expedition against the pueblo in 1696. The Picuris people abandoned the pueblo, heading east onto the Great Plains of Kansas to live with Apache allies. A decade later, the Spanish sent a party onto the Plains to encourage the Picuris people to return home, and they slowly began to trickle in.

Life for the Picuris people became increasingly harsh over the next two centuries. Diseases, Comanche raids, and other difficulties devastated Picuris, and by 1890 fewer than one hundred tribal members remained.

Contemporary Life

Today some three hundred forty people call themselves Picuris, and their situation is improving. Most residents work outside the 17,000-acre reservation at Los Alamos National Laboratories, in Taos, and in Santa Fe, where the tribe owns and operates the upscale Hotel Santa Fe. Some residents also raise alfalfa and hay, and the tribe manages timber holdings. A tribal council and a governor elected by all adults direct the pueblo's secular affairs.

Art, Crafts, and Culture

Picuris is best known in the arts community for micaceous pottery. This golden-hued pottery is made from a mica-flecked clay, fired without a glaze, which lets the clay's natural beauty shine. A handful of Picuris potters create micaceous pieces; one such talented artist is Anthony Duran.

Other artists are busy embroidering, weaving, and creating beadwork, jewelry, and sculpture. Former governor Gerald Nailor is a well-regarded painter, and Margaret Archuleta—micaceous

PICURIS

Must-see: Visitor center, the hilltop ruins

〰〰〰

January 1: various dances

January 6: King's Day honoring new officers with various dances

late January/early February (date TBA): various dances

June 17-18: annual Tri-Cultural Arts and Crafts Fair, with work by local and visiting artists and craftspeople

August 9-10: San Lorenzo Feast Days, including Catholic vespers and sunset dance on August 9, and morning foot races, a church procession, corn dances, appearances by *koshares*, and a pole climb on August 10

December 24: evening matachina dances

December 25: matachina dances

December 28: children's dances

〰〰〰

P.O. Box 127, Peñasco, NM 87533
Visitor Center, (505) 587-2519
Governor's Office, (505) 587-2957
www.picurispueblo.com

VISITING PICURIS

DIRECTIONS: Located 60 miles north of **Santa Fe**. Take US 84/285 north to **Española**, then NM 68 up the **Rio Grande Gorge** to Embudo. Turn east (right) onto NM 75 and proceed approximately thirteen miles. Turn north (left) onto either of two paved access roads that lead to the village.

VISITOR CENTER/MUSEUM: Picuris has a nice **visitor center** overlooking a fishing pond. The center includes a modest restaurant, restrooms, convenience store, small gift shop, and museum. The museum contains many interesting artifacts recovered in the 1961 archeological excavation of the Picuris ruins by the Fort Burgwin Research Center near Ranchos de Taos. The suggested admission donation to the museum is $3. The center is located just east of the Governor's Office and the church. Hours normally are 9 A.M.–5 P.M. daily.

TOURS: Self-guided or guided tours (with advance notice, $3 per person) through the pueblo's lovely church and extensive ruins, which include the former south plaza and the hilltop room blocks. Still intact is the remarkable multistory round "tower" kiva, the only such among all the pueblos. It was first erected about 1500.

PHOTOGRAPHY: Photo permits are available at the Governor's Office or the Visitor Center and cost $5 per day for still photographers, and $10 for movie and video photographers. Please inquire before photographing tribal ceremonies.

SKETCHING/SOUND RECORDING: A sketching permit is $10.

DINING: **Hidden Valley Restaurant**, located in the visitor center, serves traditional Pueblo and New Mexican fare, hamburgers, and sandwiches. The staff also can prepare group meals with advance notice. There are a few places to eat in nearby **Peñasco**.

ACCOMMODATIONS: None are available within the reservation. The tribe owns and manages the handsome **Hotel Santa Fe** in **Santa Fe**: (505) 982-1200.

CAMPING: A handful of unimproved sites with fire grills but no hookups are found at the fishing ponds. The nightly fee is $8.

RECREATION: From March through the end of October, Picuris offers **fishing** for rainbow trout in **Tutah Lake** at the Visitor Center and **Puun-na Pond** along the entry road. Pueblo rangers collect daily permit fees at the lakes; $7 for adults, $6 for seniors, $5 for children. Summer hours are 8 A.M.–6:30 P.M. Call (505) 587-1601 for details.

ARTISTS AND GALLERIES: The visitor center has a small **gift shop** that carries a selection of goods produced by Picuris artisans, notably micaceous pottery.

There are a handful of Picuris homes where local artists sell their arts and crafts, though most are open only during peak visitation times. A dozen or so residents, however, pursue an interesting range of media, and most are happy to show you their work with some advance notice.

Manual Archuleta works in oils, acrylics, ink, and colored pencil. (505) 587-2116.

Margaret Archuleta creates exquisite embroidered men's dance kilts and women's mantas (shawls), as well as micaceous wedding vases, beanpots, bowls, and animal figurines. This remarkable woman, born in 1932, has led the pueblo's efforts to pass the Tiwa language onto the next generations, and has served on many boards and councils within and outside the pueblo. P.O. Box 17, Peñasco, NM 87533. (505) 587-2166.

Caroline D. Honyumptewa works in micaceous pottery, including animal figurines, bowls, mugs, beanpots, and friendship bowls. (505) 587-0411.

John C. Keesing is a micaceous clay potter. P.O. Box 15746, Santa Fe, NM 87504.

Roberta Martinez creates miniature micaceous figurines and Christmas ornaments. P.O. Box 265, Chamisal, NM 87521.

Jess Mermejo works in micaceous clay and woven belts, and is a designated **Taos County Living Treasure**. (505) 587-0411.

Gerald Nailor produces oil and watercolor paintings, and also works in micaceous clay. P.O. Box 132, Vadito, NM 87579. (505) 587-1733.

Karen Rael produces micaceous jewelry and contemporary jewelry with precious stones. P.O. Box 265, Chamisal, NM 87521.

Daniel Vincent Sam, of Pueblo/Tlingit/Navajo heritage, chooses pencil, colored pencil, and crayon as his media. (505) 587-1077.

potter, talented textile embroiderer, and guardian of the pueblo's Tiwa language—has many admirers. The pueblo also claims sculptor Robert Dale Tsosie, of Navajo/Picuris heritage.

Picuris has long treasured its San Lorenzo Catholic church, originally built in the 1770s. In the 1980s the building was discovered to be in serious danger of collapsing. Cement plaster had been applied over the church's exterior decades earlier, but water seeping underneath this cement skin had eroded the adobe within. Conservators found that the old structure could not be saved, and so it was torn down and rebuilt on the same foundation, using traditional methods, by tribal members and non-Indian volunteers with funding provided by the New Mexico Community Foundation. The new church was rededicated in 1993. On the plaza, tribal members perform elaborate dance ceremonies and host the annual Tri-Cultural Arts and Crafts Fair on Father's Day.

POJOAQUE
(poh-HWA-kay)

Po-suwae-geh: "Water Drinking Place"

LOCATED ON A PROMONTORY above the confluence of the Rio Tesuque and Rio Nambe, on a natural travel corridor between Santa Fe and north-central New Mexico, Pojoaque has had a turbulent history. Over several centuries, armed conflicts and diseases took their toll on the pueblo's population, and Hispanic and Anglo settlers acquired most of the community's most productive farmland. During the historic era, Pojoaque was abandoned three times and at one point even ceased to function as a political and social entity.

The pueblo was permanently reestablished in 1933. Although it remains the smallest of the pueblos in land and population, its elders have taken the American free enterprise credo to heart. Pojoaque operates many successful commercial endeavors along today's busy US 84/285, and is home to the award-winning Poeh Cultural Center and Museum and a number of talented artisans.

History

The Pojoaque Valley area was settled as early as A.D. 500, and in the late fifteenth and early sixteenth centuries the area supported a large population in several major pueblos. Pojoaque tribal members participated in the Pueblo Revolt of 1680, and the pueblo was ravaged in the re-conquest and abandoned. In 1706, five families resettled the pueblo. By 1712 it had a "cosmopolitan" population of seventy-nine persons of Pueblo, Navajo, Apache, Ute, Comanche, and Spanish descent. In the nineteenth century the community suffered several devastating epidemics, including a smallpox epidemic in 1890, and again the pueblo was abandoned. Early in the twentieth century small groups attempted to reoccupy the pueblo, but these efforts proved futile, and eventually, in 1912, even the governor left to seek outside employment.

However, surviving members of the tribe sought to revive the pueblo, and in 1936 the federal government permanently conferred official tribal status on the tribe's forty or so remaining members. A tribal government was formed and the pueblo was provided with a remnant of its original land base—a scant 11,600 acres—making it the smallest pueblo in total area.

Contemporary Life

Pojoaque joined other New Mexico pueblos to capitalize on gaming when it opened its Cities of Gold Casino in 1995. The name is a sly reference to the vain quest that first brought Spanish Conquistadors to what is now northern New Mexico, and reflects the feisty nature of the pueblo's longtime governor, Jacob Viarrial. The

Cities of Gold Casino, Pojoaque
DEB FRIEDRICHS

Laboratories. Other tribal endeavors of special interest to visitors are the pueblo's handsome Poeh Cultural Center and Museum, the Cities of Gold Hotel, the Cities of Gold Sports Bar, and a golf resort. Thus, despite being the smallest in terms of population, the Pojoaque tribe is the second-largest private employer in northern New Mexico. The tribal council is open to all adult members. The council elects the governor and officials for two-year terms.

Art, Crafts, and Culture

Pojoaque is becoming a major center for Pueblo arts and arts education. The tribe numbers among its members several notable artists, including sculptor George Rivera, who also has served for many years as the tribe's lieutenant governor. Other pueblo artisans are working in traditional and contemporary styles of blackware, polychrome, and micaceous pottery, and jewelry. The pottery of Lucy Year Flower Tafoya is notable, as is the work of Thelma and Joseph Talachy and their daughter Melissa, and Gloria Golden Rod Garcia.

Pojoaque is home to the Poeh Cultural Center and Museum, which houses offices and art studios that are used for educational programs—open to Native American students only—in basket weaving, pottery, sculpture, drummaking, embroidery, and other fine and traditional arts. The center occupies a remarkable adobe building that includes a four-story round tower and other details reflective of true Pueblo architecture. The center has become a key institution in the ongoing and remarkable growth of traditional and contemporary Pueblo arts.

A 10,000-square-foot museum opens in the fall of 2002. Its third phase will include a children's museum, café, museum shop, archival research facility, and performing space.

Pueblo members resumed traditional dances in 1973 and are steadily increasing the number and range of dances that they conduct. To date, these include the buffalo, deer, butterfly, eagle, pipe, and corn dances. Members are also working to revive the native Tewa language.

right: Pow wow dancer, Pojoaque
DEB FRIEDRICHS

"gold" generated from this casino funds a wide variety of sorely needed facilities and educational, health, and social service programs for the 325 tribal members of Pojoaque, and has provided capital to launch numerous business ventures.

The tribal government recently opened the attractive Pojoaque Pueblo Wellness Center—which includes a gym, weight room, racquetball courts, and pool, as well as a library and Boys and Girls Club. The center is open to all pueblo members, and other area residents as well. The pueblo also has built a new kiva.

The tribe owns and operates the Pojoaque Pueblo Plaza Shopping Center on US 84/285, which includes a bank, laundry, hardware store, pizza restaurant, auto services shop, drug store, supermarket, food franchises, and several other businesses. The pueblo also operates a gas station and convenience center, a 99-unit apartment complex, and a 220-unit mobile home park, and is developing a business park for clients interested in the pueblo's proximity to Los Alamos National

VISITING POJOAQUE

DIRECTIONS: Located between **Santa Fe** and **Española**. From **Santa Fe**, head northwest on US 84/285, proceed 15 miles, and exit the highway at the stoplights at Gutierrez or Viarrial streets. The traditional village center is set on the ridge above the highway. Its access road, County Road 109, begins at the west end of the **Cities of Gold Casino** grounds.

VISITOR CENTER/MUSEUM: **The Pojoaque Visitor Center** doubles as an official state information center, and as such carries a wide assortment of brochures, maps, and books for travelers. Located at 96 Cities of Gold Rd. (505) 455-3460. Open fall–spring, Mon.–Sat. 9 A.M.–5:30 P.M. and Sun. 10 A.M.–4 P.M.; summer, Mon.–Fri. 9 A.M.–6 P.M. and Sun. 10 A.M.–4 P.M.

Poeh Museum visitors will see work of tribal members and artisans of the other northern pueblos. Located at 78 Cities of Gold Rd. (505) 455-3334, www.poehstore.com or www.poehcenter.com.

TOURS: None.

PHOTOGRAPHY: Not allowed at dances. Any other intention requires tribal council approval.

SKETCHING/SOUND RECORDING: Not allowed.

CASINO: **Cities of Gold Casino** with slots, poker, blackjack, craps, and bingo. Located on US 84/285. (800) 455-3313, (505) 455-3313, or www.citiesofgold.com.

DINING: **Golden Buffet**, located in the **Cities of Gold Casino**, presents daily breakfast, lunch, and dinner buffets at modest prices.

Gold Dust Restaurant, in the **Cities of Gold Hotel**, is open daily for breakfast and dinner. (505) 455-0515.

La Mesita Restaurant serves American fare such as hamburgers, chicken, and steaks. Located on US 84/285. (505) 455-2911. Open Wed.–Sun. 11 A.M.–8 P.M.

Roadrunner Café serves good New Mexican fare. (505) 455-3012.

ACCOMMODATIONS: **Cities of Gold Hotel** includes a restaurant, gift shop, conference rooms, and 125 guest rooms. Located at 10A Cities of Gold Rd., across from the Cities of Gold Casino. (877) 455-0515 or (505) 455-0515.

CAMPING: Camping is not permitted.

RECREATION: A new thirty-six-hole **championship golf course**, designed by **Hale Irwin** and **First Golf**, opened in fall 2001. The clubhouse offers food and beverage service, a pro shop, and conference space. Eventually the resort will include lodging, a tennis complex, equestrian center, and four golf courses.

ARTISTS AND GALLERIES: **Poeh Cultural Center and Museum** plans to open a fine gift shop. Meanwhile, shop on-line at the **Poeh Store** (www.poehstore.com).

A few artists maintain studio galleries. Among them are **George Rivera** and his wife, painter **Kyuhee Lee**, who own **Rivera Lee Fine Art**. Rivera is primarily a stone and bronze sculptor of traditional and contemporary Native American subjects. A graduate of the Institute of American Indian Arts of Santa Fe, he has also studied in Europe. His work is found in several major collections, and can be viewed on the grounds of the **Poeh Cultural Center**. Lee works primarily in oil paints and

monotypes, producing impressionistic landscapes. Located off County Road 109. (505) 455-3590. Open by appointment only.

The **Pojoaque Visitor Center** is also home to perhaps northern New Mexico's largest Native arts and crafts gallery. The "collectors corner" contains exceptionally fine work, such as Hopi baskets and pottery by Rose Chino of Acoma. Located at 96 Cities of Gold Rd. (505) 455-3460. Open fall–spring, Mon.–Sat. 9 A.M.–5:30 P.M. and Sun. 10 A.M.–4 P.M.; summer, 9 A.M.–6 P.M. and Sun. 10 A.M.–4 P.M. All major credit cards accepted.

The gallery carries perhaps the largest selection of Indian pottery among any of the pueblos, including works by artists from Pojoaque and other pueblos (including Santa Clara, Acoma, Santo Domingo, Zia, and Jemez), and the Hopi of Arizona. Visitors also will find colorful Navajo carved ceramic (slip-poured) work, and numerous styles of storyteller clay figurines.

Pojoaque Visitor Center has a sizeable collection of traditional and contemporary styled jewelry featuring turquoise and coral set in sterling silver. You also can find Navajo rugs; a large selection of Zuni fetishes, both strung on necklaces and freestanding, including some made from a glass and gold slag; Hopi katsina dolls, and stone and bronze sculpture.

The **Lucky Buffalo Gift Shop**, in the **Cities of Gold Casino**, carries a small, good selection of Zuni and Navajo rings, earrings, and bracelets, and horno-baked bread.

The **Little Oasis Gift Shop** (inside **Cities of Gold Hotel**) also carries a selection of arts and crafts.

SANDIA

(sahn-DEE-ah)

T'uf Shur T'ia: "Green Reed Place"

Pueblo and Sandia Mountains, Sandia, 1880
JOHN K. HILLERS

ALTHOUGH SANDIA BORDERS ALBUQUERQUE, one of the Southwest's fastest-growing cities, the pueblo did not become a significant tourist destination until the 1990s, when the tribe opened a prosperous casino on I-25. Development has been confined to a business zone along the freeway, and so Sandia's landscape and ambience remains largely unchanged. Forests of massive cottonwoods crowd the flat valley floor bordering the Rio Grande; cows graze in verdant pastures; and river water chugs through irrigation ditches to irrigate alfalfa and cornfields. To the east, amber grasslands slope

toward the jagged west face of the Sandia Mountains. The range, which often takes on a soft pink cast at sunset, reminded early Spanish immigrants of wedges of watermelons, hence the name, which means "watermelon" in Spanish.

History

Sandia was founded about 1300. When Francisco Vásquez de Coronado and his entourage entered the upper Rio Grande Valley in the late fall of 1540, the pueblo had about three thousand inhabitants.

Sandia was then one of about sixteen Tiwa-speaking pueblos located in an area stretching from Isleta to what is today Bernalillo.

Coronado's army of three hundred thirty-six soldiers and eight hundred Mexican Indian allies pitched camp on the west side of the river near a pueblo the Spanish called Alcanfor, which probably was located a few miles south of today's Coronado State Monument, alongside NM 528 at the River's Edge subdivision.

Winter hit unexpectedly hard that year. The Spanish reported they could ride a horse across the ice on the river, and Coronado ordered the inhabitants of the nearby pueblo to move out. He also sent soldiers to the other Tiwa-speaking pueblos to requisition blankets, food, and other goods for his army. The arrogance of the Spanish understandably enraged the Pueblo people, and defiant warriors from at least one neighboring pueblo—most likely Sandia—drove off a large number of the Spanish horse herd. In retaliation, Coronado ordered an attack on the pueblo. The Spanish battled their way into the village and burned it. Prisoners were lanced or burned at the stake.

Sandia also paid a price for participating in the Pueblo Revolt of 1680. Twice the Spanish torched the pueblo, and beleaguered residents finally abandoned it around 1692. Many refugees from Sandia fled to Arizona to live among the Hopi at Payupki. In 1748 the Spanish allowed about four hundred and forty tribal members to return home. The pueblo then became a target for raiding Apache, Comanche, and Navajo war parties. A truce among the tribes was finally established at "Friendship Arroyo" near Placitas. Representatives at the parlay dug a hole, spat in it, dropped in half-smoked cigarettes, and vowed never to fight one another again. Still the pueblo's difficulties persisted, and by 1900 its population hit a low of seventy-four people.

Contemporary Life

Since the 1940s, with on-reservation financial opportunities limited to farming and livestock grazing, most of Sandia's adults have found employment in Albuquerque. Electricity did not arrive in the pueblo until 1952. Circumstances changed radically in 1984, when the pueblo opened a casino along I-25. Income from gaming has been used to improve housing, and build a gymnasium and fitness center and a wastewater treatment plant. Gaming money also supports K–12 and higher education scholarships, health care, elder, and youth programs for the tribe's approximately four hundred residents. The tribe also owns and operates Sandia Lakes Recreation Area, a rustic retreat with lakes and hiking trails in the riverside cottonwood bosque.

In 2001, the tribe opened an attractive 210,000-square-foot casino and 3,000-seat amphitheater on the grasslands facing the Sandia Mountains. Future plans include a resort hotel. The 22,877-acre reservation includes 1,700 acres of farmland and 1,900 acres of grazing land. Another tribal asset is a major arts-and-crafts sales center, Bien Mur. In all, the tribe employs more than eighteen hundred people.

VISITING SANDIA

DIRECTIONS: Located between **Albuquerque** and **Bernalillo**. To get to the village center, take Exit 234 off I-25 and head west on NM 556 two miles. Turn north (right) onto NM 313 and proceed north 3 miles to the entrance sign on your right.

VISITOR CENTER/MUSEUM: None.

TOURS: None.

PHOTOGRAPHY: Not allowed in the village. Contact the **Governor's Office** for further details.

SKETCHING/SOUND RECORDING: Not allowed.

CASINO: The new **Sandia Casino**, which opened in May 2001, offers slots, blackjack, poker, craps, roulette, keno, and bingo in a beautiful, crescent-shaped building of Pueblo-style architecture, featuring 40-foot-high panoramic windows, cut stone, and pueblo art (including tiles made by Sandia children). It also houses a lounge. Exit 234 on I-25, on the northeast

corner of I-25 and Tramway Boulevard. (800) 526-9366, (505) 897-2173.

DINING: The **casino** offers several dining options, including an upscale restaurant with table service, a buffet restaurant, a coffee shop, and a deli.

ACCOMMODATIONS: A casino resort hotel is planned.

CAMPING: Camping is not permitted.

RECREATION: **Sandia Lakes Recreation Area** is a pretty spot that offers fishing and quiet hiking trails that wind through the cottonwood forest, which lines the east bank of the Rio Grande. The area is home to abundant wildlife. During spring and fall, look for geese and ducks. Other bird life includes blue herons, bald eagles, and numerous songbirds. (505) 897-3971.

Three small lakes hold rainbow trout, catfish, and smallmouth bass. Bait and tackle are available in a convenience shop. Nearby are a playground and picnic areas. The lakes are located just off NM 313, one mile north of NM 556.

The Sandia reservation also has a 107-acre **Buffalo Preserve**, with more than twenty bison. Look for them from a vantage point at the **Bien Mur Market Center**. Viewing is free.

ARTISTS AND GALLERIES: The **Bien Mur Market Center** is the largest tribally owned arts-and-crafts shop among the pueblos. Its huge inventory includes a wide assortment of jewelry and pottery, katsinas, paintings, baskets, animal fetishes, folk art, and leather crafts drawn from all nineteen pueblos. Also included are works by Navajo artisans, including textiles, and work by Hopi artisans. Traditional dance sashes, shawls, and leggings, Pendleton blankets, handmade knives, flutes, rattles, and music CDs are also available. The round, kiva-shaped facility adjoins the tribe's buffalo preserve. Located on the southeast corner of I-25 and Tramway Boulevard. Open Mon.–Sat. 9 A.M.–5:30 P.M. and Sun. 11 A.M.–5 P.M. (800) 365-5400 or www.bienmur.com.

The **casino gift shop** also offers a selection of arts and crafts.

The tribal government also has been engaged in a protracted legal dispute regarding the reservation's historic boundaries. The tribe believes its original Spanish land grant extended to the top of the Sandia Mountains, revered by tribal members. Most of this mountain terrain, containing their most sacred shrines, was incorporated into Cibola National Forest.

Art, Crafts, and Culture

Despite their tumultuous past, the Sandia people retain most of their traditional cultural, social, and religious practices, and some residents are actively reviving old arts and crafts. The people of Sandia are among the few Pueblo groups who weave willow and yucca baskets. Other artisans work in traditional redware and new ceramic-style pottery forms. Still others embroider and weave belts, make jewelry, and create heishi (traditional beadwork).

San Antonio de Padua church, with its gracefully curved front facade, is found in the north end of the village.

SAN FELIPE

(sahn fay-LEE-pay)

Indian name uncertain

PERHAPS THE LEAST-VISITED of all the pueblos, San Felipe is tucked away in a little valley on the west bank of the Rio Grande, obscured from the view of passing motorists on I-40 by a series of low hills. Like their Pueblo neighbors, the people of San Felipe maintain a low profile. The San Felipe corn dance in May, an arts and crafts fair, and the community's adobe church draw a few serious tourists each year, but the tribe's casino and retail complex on I-25 are the pueblo's main attractions today.

Each May, in a plaza worn into a vast bowl over the centuries by countless shuffling feet, the rhythms of corn dancers and singers roll over the river and echo from the walls of the black volcanic mesa that looms above the village. Watching this prayerful ceremony for a successful harvest, visitors are transported back in time and the cares of the modern world recede.

History

The San Felipe people belong to the Keres language group, which migrated south to the great plateaus that flank the Jemez Mountains' eastern rim. In the early fourteenth century, they moved off the plateaus and down to the banks of the Rio Grande, establishing a village called Katishtya. This village was relocated several times, finally settling on the present site on the west bank of the river in the early 1700s.

The people of San Felipe participated in the Pueblo Revolt of 1680 and then, fearing a counterattack, retreated to a fortified pueblo on a Jemez

left: Spinning wool, San Felipe, 1900
MARY E. DISSETTE

mesa top. The following year exiled Governor Antonio de Otermin made a foray back up the river from El Paso, found the pueblo of San Felipe deserted, and ordered it burned. In 1692, Don Diego de Vargas found the former residents of San Felipe still living in their mesa top redoubt, and he persuaded them to come down in peace. Franciscan priests baptized more than a hundred children born during the interim, and thereafter the San Felipe people remained loyal to the Spanish crown. They even cooperated with Spanish authorities in punitive expeditions against other pueblos, including Jemez, Acoma, and Zuni.

A 1776 census reported a pueblo population of 406, but in the following century disease claimed a third of their number.

SAN FELIPE

Must-see: Church, old plaza

January 6: King's Day, with corn dances

May 1: San Felipe Feast Day, with major green-corn dances

June 29: San Pedro Feast Day

October or early December: annual San Felipe Arts and Crafts Fair

P.O. Box 4339, San Felipe Pueblo, NM 87001 Governor's Office, (505) 867-3381

VISITING SAN FELIPE

DIRECTIONS: Located between **Albuquerque** and **Santa Fe**. To reach the village center, from Albuquerque head north on I-25 for 26 miles to Exit 252, and then head west on the pueblo access road for 3 miles, crossing to the west bank of the Rio Grande.

VISITOR CENTER/MUSEUM: None.

TOURS: None.

PHOTOGRAPHY: Not allowed.

SKETCHING/SOUND RECORDING: Not allowed.

CASINO: **Casino Hollywood** plays roulette, craps, poker, blackjack and slots. Located at Exit 252 off I-25. (505) 867-6700.

DINING: **San Felipe Pueblo Restaurant** serves breakfast all day (including omelettes, huevos rancheros, pancakes), gourmet hamburgers and sandwiches, salads, Pueblo specialties, New Mexican food, pasta, and other dinner favorites.

Located within the **Travel Center** at Exit 252 on I-25. (505) 867-4706. Open daily 6 A.M.–10 P.M.

The **R and T 4 Way Shopper and Grill** serves hamburgers and sandwiches. It also stocks snacks, pop, and convenience items. Located on pueblo access road, on the east side of the river at the village's four-way stop sign.

Casino Hollywood has a buffet-style dining room that serves a good breakfast, lunch, and dinner at reasonable prices.

ACCOMMODATIONS: Not available, but **Albuquerque** offers many hotel options.

CAMPING: Camping is not permitted.

RECREATION: Not available.

ARTISTS AND GALLERIES: **West Turquoise Trail** is an intriguing shop run by **Dora and Robert Garcia**. Their daughter Geraldine contributes sterling silver jewelry. The shop carries a large selection of Pendleton blankets,

Kaibab moccasins, and occasionally pottery produced by one of the pueblo's few potters. Located 1 mile west on the pueblo access road. Exit 252 off I-25. (505) 867-4959. Open summer, 9 A.M.–8 P.M. and otherwise, 9 A.M.–6 P.M. Major credit cards are accepted.

Consider making arrangements to view the work of individual artists, such as **Darrell Candelaria**, a notable young potter who works in almost any Pueblo decorative style: polychrome, black-on-white, red-on-cream, geometrics, naturalistics, corrugated, or carved. His most remarkable works read like a Pueblo pottery sampler, with examples of all styles incorporated on different sections of a single vessel. (505) 867-0653.

The **Travel Center Gift Shop** offers a fine selection of Indian arts and crafts from the region, including moccasins from San Felipe and animal fetishes from Zuni. There are also sterling silver bracelets and pottery in various styles and forms. Located at exit 252 off I-25.

Contemporary Life

Today, San Felipe has a population of close to twenty-five hundred. A land base of 48,930 acres supports some farming, but most residents work off the reservation. Many people own homes outside the traditional village core.

The tribe has begun some commercial endeavors along busy I-25, which borders the reservation. This includes a casino, and a gas station and traveler's center with showers, a convenience store, TV lounge, restaurant, and gift shop. Other developments are planned.

Art, Crafts, and Culture

About a dozen artists reside at San Felipe, including Sara Candelaria, who produces storyteller figures and nativity scenes, and talented young Darrell Candelaria. At least three families are producing *heishi* (handmade beads), and one tribal member makes moccasins.

The church at San Felipe was built in the early eighteenth century and is an outstanding example of mission architecture. The pueblo's feast day of San Felipe, highlighted by a large green-corn dance, is popular with Indian and non-Indian visitors alike.

SAN ILDEFONSO

(sahn eel-deh-FOHN-so)

Po-woh-ge: "Where the Water Cuts Through"

Feast day, San Ildefonso
STEPHEN TRIMBLE

OF THE PUEBLOS NEAREST SANTA FE, San Ildefonso is one of the most popular with visitors and art collectors. The traditional pueblo village is scenic, and features many shops and galleries where residents display fine pottery and other goods.

The pueblo's large central plaza, divided into two areas with separate kivas, is a wonderful place to observe a ceremonial dance. An enormous, ancient cottonwood tree provides a shady respite in summer for visitors who are savvy enough to get there early.

The pueblo enjoys a breathtaking setting. To the west flows the Rio Grande, which dips into the mouth of spectacular White Rock Canyon south of the pueblo. Across the river rise the tiered mesas of the Pajarito Plateau, and the looming Jemez Mountains. To the north rises the distinctive knob Black Mesa; be sure to notice the rim, which is pockmarked with caves. Monstrous ogres live in these caves, or so Pueblo mothers tell their children. If the children misbehave, the ogres will come down, snatch them up, take them back to their lair, and eat them!

SAN ILDEFONSO

Must-see: Tribal museum, several
art galleries, a dance ceremony

〰〰〰

The pueblo hosts a year round schedule of
ceremonials and dances, some of which are
open to the public while others are closed.

Among events the public may attend are
corn dances in June, August and September
(dates vary from year to year).

The major ceremony open to the
public is the annual feast day on January 23,
when the buffalo and Comanche dances
are presented.

〰〰〰

Rt. 5, Box 315-A, Santa Fe, NM 87501
(505) 455-2273
Governor's Office, (505) 455-3549

History

The Tewa-speaking San Ildefonso people trace
their origins to the area around Mesa Verde
National Park in southwestern Colorado. Those
ancestors who migrated from there to the canyons
of the Pajarito Plateau settled in several villages,
Tynonyi, Navawi, Otowi, and Tsankawi. The
latter site is preserved within Bandelier National
Monument and is publicly accessible. The present
village may date back as far as the 1300s. In 1591, a
Spanish expedition reported that some two thousand
people resided here in a multistory compound.

The first Catholic mission was established at
the pueblo in 1617, but the church was destroyed
in the Pueblo Revolt of 1680. In 1694, Diego de
Vargas sought to bring the pueblo back under
Spanish dominion. The residents retreated to the
top of Black Mesa, where they withstood an
extended siege. At last the combatants agreed to
terms, and the proud pueblo members returned
to their village below.

Sadly, the next two hundred fifty years were
disastrous for the pueblo. A lethal bout of Spanish
flu after World War I reduced the pueblo's
population to ninety people. The pueblo lost a
large portion of its land base as well.

Contemporary Life

From that low point, San Ildefonso has experienced
a gradual but continual revival, fueled to a great
extent by the power of art. In 1908 a Pueblo woman,
Maria Povenka (Yellow Pond Lily) Martinez,
obtained some potsherds from her husband Julian,
who was working with Dr. Edgar Lee Hewett on

an excavation of pueblo ruins in the Pajarito canyons nearby. He suggested she try to reproduce the unusual work. Maria, a maker of everyday pottery used in the village, succeeded. During the next few decades she became a world-renowned "ambassador" of Pueblo culture to the world. Maria was a popular participant in the 1915 San Diego World's Fair, and fairs in Chicago in 1933 and San Francisco in 1939. Around 1919, Maria and Julian perfected what would become the trademark San Ildefonso pottery, the lovely blackware (created by smothering the fire with manure or fine woody materials).

The resulting interest in her work helped spark a general revival of Pueblo pottery-making throughout her pueblo and New Mexico as a whole, which in turn led to increased exposure and success for Pueblo jewelers and other Pueblo artists.

Today, many of San Ildefonso's more than six hundred residents make their living creating and selling arts and crafts. In fact, this is about the only economic activity here, because the tribal government is opposed to the gaming business and does not promote tourism. Most of the 26,000-acre San Ildefonso land base remains undeveloped. The tribe's only significant business endeavor is a service station and convenience market on NM 502, and so most adults work off the reservation.

Husking corn, San Ildefonso, 1935
T. Harmon Parkhurst

VISITING SAN ILDEFONSO

DIRECTIONS: Located 24 miles northwest of **Santa Fe**. From Santa Fe, head north on US 84/285 for 19 miles and turn west onto NM 502. Proceed 6 miles and turn north (right) onto the village access road (BIA 401) and proceed to the visitor center.

VISITOR CENTER/MUSEUM: The pueblo's **Tewa Visitor Center** offers historic photos of the village and displays of arts and crafts including its famous pottery, paintings, and jewelry. Located on the pueblo entrance road. (505) 455-3549. Open daily, 8 A.M.–5 P.M. Admission is $3 per auto or $10 per bus, plus 50 cents per person. The pueblo closes at 5 P.M.

San Ildefonso Tribal Museum offers an informative display on the traditional pottery process, from mixing the clay to firing the vessel. Works by many of the pueblo's famous potters, including the renowned Maria Martinez and her husband Julian, and Blue Corn Calabaza, are featured. Historic photos and examples of other Pueblo arts and crafts—black and white *mantas* (shawls), moccasins, ribbon shirts, and leather works—round out the exhibits. Adjoins the Governor's Office northwest of the plaza. Open weekdays 8 A.M.–4 P.M. Admission is free.

PHOTOGRAPHY: Still camera permits cost $10 a day. A video camera permit is $20. Respect all "keep off" signs on the kivas; entrance to the church grounds is forbidden.

SKETCHING/SOUND RECORDING: A sketching permit is $25. Sound recording is not allowed.

DINING: Nearest options are in **Española**, 15 minutes away, or Pojoaque.

ACCOMMODATIONS: Many options are available in nearby **Española** or **Santa Fe**.

CAMPING: Camping is not permitted, but guests are welcome to picnic at the fishing ponds.

RECREATION: The pueblo maintains small **fishing ponds**, open daily 8 A.M.–4 P.M. in winter, otherwise 8 A.M.–5 P.M. Pay for permit on site. Swimming is not allowed. Hiking to the Rio Grande, Black Mesa, or other parts of the reservation is not allowed.

ARTISTS AND GALLERIES: Aguilar Shop has been in business since the 1960s and carries pottery, acrylic and watercolor paintings by **Alfred Aguilar** and Zuni and Santo Domingo jewelry. Particularly popular are the clay buffalos with rough hides in black, red, and polychrome. The family also produces storytellers and Nativity sets. Located next to the visitor center. Mailing address is Rt. 5, Box 318C, Santa Fe, NM 87501. Credit cards accepted.

Gonzales Shop features the exquisite pottery of **John Gonzales**. He specializes in plates 4–20 inches in diameter, sometimes set with heishi, turquoise, lapis, coral, and even diamonds. Ceramic stains provide for precise designs, often featuring feather patterns or the water serpent. His web site also has links to a few other San Ildefonso potters, including Maria Martinez and Eric Sunbird Fender. Located on the south side of the plaza. (505) 455-2476 or www.sanildefonso.com. E-mail at saninative@aol.com.

Kalavaza Pottery features works by **Seashell Flower** and her brother **Krieg Kalavaza**, offspring of famed potters **Blue Corn** and **Santiago**. Their residence, filled with a dazzling display of baskets and pottery, has served as a gallery for more than thirty years. The duo produces work in more than twenty different colors, including rare green, yellow, and dark brown, in prehistoric, historic, and contemporary styles. Their favorite media are polychrome, black and white, and black on black, but they also produce micaceous pottery with orange designs. Buyers also may place custom orders. Located on the south side of the plaza. (505) 455-7496.

Martinez Family Gallery carries pottery and jewelry produced by family members, some Hopi katsinas by **Robert Harris**, and dance regalia in shell (such as arm bands and chokers) and traditional gourd rattles. **Juan Rey Martinez** produces silver jewelry while his sister **Alice** works in black pottery. Located off the plaza on the north side of the village. (505) 455-2872. Open 8 A.M.–5 P.M. in summer and 9 A.M.–4 P.M. other times. Credit cards accepted.

Bob Peña Shop features fine arts and crafts from San Ildefonso and other pueblos. Jewelry includes Hopi overlay, Navajo silver bracelets, Zuni cufflinks, and Santo Domingo heishi and coral work. There are belt buckles, watchbands, pendants, squash blossoms, and bolos. In pottery, look for work from Zia; deep-carved pieces from Santa Clara; redware and red and tan pieces items from Jemez; cast, deep carved and horsehair styles from Acoma, and multicolored poured and carved Navajo work. There also are beaded moccasins from Oklahoma and beaded berets. Located on the east side of the plaza. (505) 455-3758. Open daily but call first.

Sandra's Pottery contains examples of black, red, brown, and gray pottery, usually with feather motifs. Located off the plaza just northwest of the Governor's Office. (505) 455-1197. Open Mon.–Sat. 9 A.M.–4 P.M. Cash or checks only.

Sunbeam is a family business that concentrates on pottery and clay sculpture produced by heirs of **Maria Martinez: Barbara** and **Robert Gonzales** and children **Cavan, Aaron, Brandan,** and **Derek. Barbara** produces award-winning vessels with a trademark spider web motif set with inlaid turquoise and coral after firing. **Robert** creates animal figurines, including polished bears and turtles. **Cavan** produces large polychrome bowls, while Aaron is known for black buffalo and unusual black ram heads. The shop also sells Navajo, Hopi, and Zuni jewelry. Located on the east side of plaza. (505) 455-7132. Open daily year round, 9 A.M.–4 P.M. Major credit cards accepted.

Torres Gallery, founded in 1990 with a focus on San Ildefonso pottery, today sells delightful turtles by **Eugene Gutierrez** and black-on-black, redware, and polychrome work created by **Elvis "Tsee-Pin" Torres**. Torres also creates "clay wash" paintings using red, black, tan and terracotta clay slips. Katsinas carved by **Alan Cruz** (Hopi/ San Juan), and a selection of drawings, prints, and paintings are available, including works by **Paul Vigil** of Tesuque. Also for sale are jewelry pieces by Navajo and Pueblo artisans. Located on the east side of the plaza. (505) 455-7547. Open daily year round, 8 A.M.–5 P.M. Credit cards are accepted.

Buffalo dancers, San Ildefonso
STEPHEN TRIMBLE

Art, Crafts, and Culture

The black-on-black pottery first developed by Maria and Julian, which features alternating lustrous and matte finishes, became the signature style of San Ildefonso, and propelled Maria's vessels to the status of fine collectors items. Today, individual pieces of her work can sell for upward of six figures, placing Maria Martinez in the highest echelon of American artists.

While the pueblo popularized blackware, other forms of pottery also were developed to complement the ebony-like work, and today San Ildefonso artists produce beautiful redware and polychrome vessels in both carved and smooth forms, figurines, and other types of pottery. One of the most common designs found on San Ildefonso pottery is the Avanyu or water serpent, whose rippling spine and forked tongue represent roiling summer rain clouds and lightning, respectively.

Maria's son Popovi Da and her grandson Tony Da continued to break new ground with their pottery, and it was they who introduced the technique of setting stones into works after firing them. Many other families have emerged as artistic dynasties as well, including the family of Blue Corn Calabaza. San Ildefonso potters also have shown a remarkable level of accomplishment and willingness to experiment: John Gonzales produces finely executed plates, some of which are set with precious stones, including diamonds. Eric Sunbird creates rare black-on-green work. Potter Russell Sanchez incorporates turquoise, coral, and shell heishi into medium-sized vessels with finishes of black, brown, and varying shades of red.

The pueblo's attractive adobe San Ildefonso church was built between 1957 and 1968. It is open for services every Saturday at 6:30 P.M. and Sunday morning.

SAN JUAN

(Sahn HUAhn)

Ohkay Owingeh: "Village of the Strong People"

BENEATH BLACK MESA, at the confluence of the Rio Grande and the Rio Chama, lies San Juan Pueblo. Framed by the graceful curves of the Jemez Mountains to the west and the jagged Truchas Peaks of the Sangre de Cristo Mountains to the east, this humble pueblo has witnessed an amazing number of New Mexico's most important historic events. And the community continues to make history.

Site of the first Spanish settlement in New Mexico in 1598 and birthplace of Po'Pay (Popé), who led the Pueblo Revolt of 1680, San Juan currently operates a number of prosperous businesses and is one of northern New Mexico's major employers.

It is also home to many artists, particularly those who specialize in carved redware pottery. With an active spiritual and ceremonial life, San Juan people have blended the strengths of the past with a promising future.

Redware pot
by Reycita Garcia, San Juan
MARK NOHL

History

San Juan was first occupied in the late twelfth century. The capital of a Pueblo province, it was also the center of a meeting ground called Yunque-Owinge. According to tribal authorities, only a Yunque-Owinge native could commit all of the pueblos to war, and such a declaration could only be made at Yunque-Owinge. This would prove prophetic.

When Don Juan de Oñate led a weary band of settlers, soldiers, Mexican Indians, and Franciscan priests into the area in August 1598, he was so impressed with the industry and friendliness of the native people that he named their pueblo San Juan de los Caballeros (Saint John of the Gentlemen). He decided the site would serve as the first capital of the vast new Spanish territory of Nuevo Mexico, which stretched from Texas to the Pacific Ocean and north into what is now Utah and Colorado. For the capital, he chose an Ancestral Pueblo village site on the west bank of the Rio Grande, opposite Ohkay Owingeh, called Yunque, which he renamed San Gabriel. The settlers dug a major irrigation ditch first, and then they began work on the Catholic church.

In 1608, the governor decided to re-establish the capital in a new, uninhabited location, which became Santa Fe. San Gabriel was eventually abandoned, and its foundations are now buried under shifting sands and fields of alfalfa. Today only scattered potsherds and a small metal plaque identify the site, which nonetheless is one of America's most important historic landmarks. (To see the plaque, drive west across the bridge over the Rio Grande, turn left onto Yunque Owinge Road, and look for the marker on a low hill on the left.)

right: Deer dancer, San Juan, 1935
T. HARMON PARKHURST

Deer dancer, San Juan
STEPHEN TRIMBLE

By 1680, the presence of the Spanish among the Rio Grande Valley pueblos had become unbearable. Thousands of Pueblo people were forced into labor to pay taxes due the Spanish Crown, and Pueblo wealth—what little there was—was confiscated. Traditional religious practices were banned.

A priest from San Juan named Po'Pay (Ripe Pumpkin) became a bitter foe of the Spanish after he and a dozen other religious figures were flogged for conducting traditional ceremonies. He and other confederates, including Tagu of San Juan and leaders from other pueblos, dared to plot an armed rebellion against Spain, which was then the world's most powerful nation. The Spanish learned of the plan from informants and moved to seize Po'Pay, but he eluded capture and took refuge at Taos, where he finalized plans for the armed revolt.

On August 10, 1680, all of the New Mexico pueblos except Isleta, and the Hopi of Arizona rose up simultaneously and attacked Spanish positions.

Churches were burned, priests killed, and roughly one thousand settlers slain. The surviving Spanish fled to Santa Fe and took refuge in the Palace of the Governors. When pueblo warriors cut off the palace's water supply and laid siege, Governor Otermin ordered the territory to be abandoned. Fighting their way out of the palace grounds, the Spanish beat a hasty retreat down the Rio Grande Valley, stopping briefly at Isleta before moving on to El Paso.

Twelve years later, Don Juan de Vargas led an expedition that reasserted Spanish control over Nuevo Mexico, and the people of San Juan grudgingly learned to live with the foreigners in their midst. In 1998, Spanish vice-president Francisco Alvarez-Cascos visited San Juan to mark the quincentenary of the founding of San Gabriel and Spain's role in this region. In a historic ceremony, Pueblo and Spanish leaders spoke of their admiration for one another, and reaffirmed their mutual desire to live in prosperity and peace.

DIRECTIONS: Located 26 miles northwest of **Santa Fe**, on **Española's** northern edge. To reach the pueblo village, head north from Española on NM 68 for 1 mile. Turn west (left) onto NM 74 just past the casino, and proceed 1 mile to the village center.

VISITOR CENTER/MUSEUM: None (planning is underway for the First Capital Heritage Center on NM 68).

TOURS: Guided tours of the **Bison Park** and the **historic San Gabriel site** can be arranged. For details call (505) 852-4400.

PHOTOGRAPHY: Generally not permitted, but check with Governor's Office.

SKETCHING/SOUND RECORDING: Not permitted.

CASINO: **Ohkay Casino** offers blackjack, craps, and roulette, and more than five hundred slots. The casino includes a bar and also sponsors major boxing events and rodeos in adjoining facilities. Located on NM 68 just north of Española. (800) PLAY-AT-OK or www.ohkay.com.

DINING: **Harvest Café**, located in the casino, features inexpensive, all-you-can-eat buffet breakfast, lunch, and dinner dining. Española has many options, including the outstanding **El Paragua**: (505) 753-3211.

ACCOMMODATIONS: **Ohkay Resort**, which adjoins the casino, includes a **Best Western** hotel with a pool and lovely views of nearby mountain ranges. Rates range from $55 nightly for a basic double room midweek to $125 for a suite on a holiday. (877) 829-2865.

CAMPING: **Ohkay RV Park** has 84 sites, showers and restrooms, a laundry, and convenience store. Reservations and check-in are conducted at the convenience store. Rates for RV sites with hookups for electricity, water, and sewer are $21 per night or $110 per week for two adults and one child. Extra guests are an additional $1 each per night. Tent sites cost $10 per night, or $15 with hookups. Located in north **Española** just off NM 68 at 2016 Riverside Dr./ P.O. Box 1079, San Juan Pueblo, NM 87566. (505) 753-5067.

RECREATION: Fishing for bluegill, catfish, and bass in warm weather, and trout in cooler weather, is available at **San Juan Lakes**. Permits are $8 for adults, and $5 for children twelve or younger and seniors fifty-five or older. The lakes, which are located adjacent to the RV park just off NM 68 in north Española, are the site of a fishing derby every March. Bait and tackle (but no pole rentals) are available at a convenience store. For details, call (505) 753-5067.

ARTISTS AND GALLERIES: One of the top arts-and-crafts shops found in any of the nineteen pueblos is **Oke Oweenge Crafts Cooperative**. Begun in 1968 by a handful of women, today it carries a variety of work produced by more than one hundred artisans, most but not all of whom are from San Juan. You'll find a large selection of pottery, including micaceous, and the pueblo's most distinctive work—the lustrous, incised redware. A good selection of jewelry is also available, including many styles of attractive but inexpensive necklaces (less than $20) adorned with an astounding variety of seeds; traditional arm and leg rattles made of shells on leather; turquoise rings; necklaces of shell, coral and beads; bolo ties; and pierced earrings.

Look also for an attractive selection of woven goods, including embroidered kilts, sashes, and belts, as well as embroidered pillows, hairpins, vests, and commercial T-shirts.

You can also find wooden flutes, handmade moccasins that feature white leather and black soles produced in San Felipe, traditional dried foods and recipe booklets produced by **Pueblo Harvest Foods**, drawings by **Norman Pacheco**, large drums, gourd art, Christmas ornaments, beaded leather pouches and necklaces, and belt buckles.

The co-op produces a mail order catalog, serves as an artist referral center, and has a small exhibition area featuring historic photos and cultural artifacts. It is located in the village center on NM 74. (505) 852-2372. Open summer weekdays, 9 A.M.–5 P.M., and fall–spring weekdays, 9 A.M.–4:30 P.M. Credit cards accepted.

San Juan also has a few private art galleries, including **Aquino's** and **Norman Pacheco's Native American Fine Arts**, both of which are located on the pueblo entrance road, and **Sunrise Crafts** (owned by a non-tribal family), which is next to Oke Oweenge Cooperative.

San Juan native **Evelyn Quintana** is one of the few Pueblo embroiderers still active. She lives in Albuquerque. (505) 294-4100.

Contemporary Life

Today, San Juan continues to be a center of government. The largest of the six Tewa-speaking pueblos, with more than two thousand members and a reservation covering 12,230 acres, San Juan is home to the Bureau of Indian Affairs Northern Pueblos Agency, and to the Eight Northern Indian Pueblos Council (ENIPC). ENIPC coordinates an array of programs among the pueblos of San Juan, Taos, Picuris, Santa Clara, San Ildefonso, Pojoaque, Nambe, and Tesuque, ranging from education, health, and social services to economic development.

San Juan has excelled economically in the past decade. Its development entity, Tsay (Eagle) Corporation, oversees a tribal casino and resort; a gas station and travel center; an RV park; recreational lakes; and construction, roofing, cabinet, and furniture companies. The corporation is one of northern New Mexico's major private employers.

Also operating within the reservation is Ohkay T'owa Gardens, a project of the San Juan Agricultural

Cooperative, which was founded in 1992 to help revive the pueblo's agricultural traditions. Hay, alfalfa, tomatoes, corn, chiles, melons, apples, cut flowers, and herbs are grown on about two hundred acres that are irrigated with waters from the Rio Grande. A subsidiary, Pueblo Harvest Foods, produces dried and processed food products from crops raised, including dried green chile stew, dried green chile, smoked and dried tomatoes, dried apples, black bean stew, and chicos. Chicos are small corn kernels that have been lightly roasted in a horno (the traditional, wood-fired outdoor adobe ovens). They can be used in stews and soups. For wholesale and retails orders call (505) 747-3146 or visit the web site, www.puebloharvest.com.

San Juan's governor administers day-to-day external affairs and is appointed to one-year terms. Members of the tribal council serve for life.

Art, Crafts, and Culture

San Juan's artisans are perhaps best known for their lovely redware pottery, which is coveted by knowledgeable collectors around the world. Thin, geometric patterns—as well as scallops, spirals, steps, water serpents, and feathers—are incised into the bowls, vases, pots, and other forms with knives or awls before the initial firing. The lustrous red finish is achieved by rubbing the reddish clay with animal fat after the first firing, and then firing it a second time. San Juan potters also produce a number of other styles, including handsome blackware and a distinct form featuring a polished red bottom and top rim divided by a tan, incised band.

In addition to pottery, artisans are active in weaving belts, embroidering, carving stone and wood, painting, and making jewelry, particularly necklaces made of strung corn, melon, and pumpkin seeds. Native son Mike Romero, who shows at Blue Rain Gallery in Taos, produces silver and gold jewelry set with coral, turquoise, and other semiprecious stones. San Juan is one of the few pueblos where traditional willow baskets are woven.

At the physical and spiritual heart of the village are two churches: The cut-stone chapel of Nuestra Señora de Lourdes, built in 1898, and the redbricked San Juan Bautista church, built in 1913.

The San Juan people divide the physical world into three concentric circles. The inner circle encompasses the village and nearby lands and is the realm of the women. The middle ring takes in the surrounding hills and mesas and is the realm of both men and women. The land beyond the third circle is the exclusive realm of men, who hunt and provide protection from hostile forces.

SAN JUAN

Must-see: Oke Oweenge Crafts Cooperative; if possible, tour San Gabriel

January 6: King's Day, with various dances to honor the new tribal officers

late January: cloud or basket dance

late February: deer dance

June 13: corn dance

June 24: San Juan Feast Day with Comanche dance

late September: harvest dance

December 24 (evening): Catholic vespers followed by procession through village and midnight mass

December 25: all day matachina dance, evening dance

December 26: turtle dances all day

Governor's Office, P.O. Box 1099, San Juan Pueblo, NM 87566
(505) 852-4400
www.indianpueblo.org/sanjuan.html

SANTA ANA

(SAHN-tah-AH-na)

Tamaya

AMONG THE MOST ECONOMICALLY active of the nineteen pueblos is the relatively small Santa Ana. Located just 16 miles north of Albuquerque, the pueblo has capitalized on its proximity to the city by developing a range of businesses, including world-class tourism facilities. The Hyatt Regency chose to open its first major resort in New Mexico on a beautiful reservation site with views of the majestic Rio Grande Valley and west face of the Sandia Mountains.

The tribe's popular casino, golf courses, and four-star Prairie Star Restaurant are the primary attractions for visitors, but the reservation also has a beautiful picnic site at dramatic Jemez Canyon. The traditional village is also special, but is seldom open to the public.

History

The Santa Ana people believe they originated from a subterranean world to the north. Assisted by their mother, Iyatiko, they ascended through four worlds—the white, red, blue, and yellow—before emerging at Sipapu into this, the fifth world. They moved south to a place called White House (perhaps Mesa Verde), where they began to quarrel among themselves and the katsinam. When the people broke into different factions, an angry Iyatiko caused them to speak in different languages as well. One group migrated farther south to establish the historic Santa Ana village known as Tamaya on the Jemez River in the sixteenth century.

Warriors from Santa Ana participated in the Pueblo Revolt of 1680, and their pueblo was attacked and burned when the Spanish retaliated in 1687. In a battle at Zia Pueblo the next year, more Santa Ana warriors perished. When the Spanish returned permanently in 1692, the Santa Ana people

A Santa Ana man, 1925
EDWARD S. CURTIS

acquiesced to Spanish rule. The tribe even assisted the Spanish in a successful attack on the Jemez Pueblo village of Astialakwa in 1694.

Contemporary Life

The Santa Ana people are among the most enterprising of all the pueblos. With the opening of the Santa Ana Star Casino in 1994, the pueblo gained a measure of financial clout, and has leveraged this into several other successful business endeavors.

Most prominent are the tribe's golf courses: a twenty-seven-hole course open to the general public and the new Hyatt Regency Resort's eighteen hole course. Many New Mexican families make great use of the tribe's twenty-two-field soccer complex.

Santa Ana Agricultural Enterprises includes a Native American foods business, the Cooking Post.

This company produces a line of tribally grown blue corn products under the Tamaya Blue label. These include cornbread and pancake mixes, atole (corn slightly roasted before milling), and parched corn (whole kernels lightly salted). The company also sells fine corn meal to cosmetic companies. The business provides income and jobs, and puts the tribe's water rights to work to ensure their continuation. (888) 867-5198 or www.cookingpost.com.

The tribe also runs a wholesale/retail nursery of Southwestern native plants, and a T-shirt and apparel company called Warrior Apparel.

The Santa Ana reservation encompasses about 79,000 acres. This includes the original Spanish land grant around the historic village, and an additional 5,000 acres the tribe purchased in the Rio Grande Valley. Few people live year round in the historic village of Tamaya, but this ancient pueblo comes alive for ceremonial events.

Most of the more than seven hundred tribal members live in a newer village called Ranchitos on the east side of the Rio Grande, just north of Bernalillo. This village is located on the edge of beautiful meadows and great riverside marshes and bosques of native cottonwoods. Irrigation ditches deliver life-giving waters to fields and orchards. Fifty years of ill-advised flood control efforts have dramatically altered the character and ecological balance of Rio Grande's riverside bosques, but Santa Ana has committed several million dollars to restore six miles of riverway that cut through its lands.

Art, Crafts, and Culture

A handful of Santa Ana women work in embroidery, belt weaving, jewelry, pottery, and the creation of ceremonial ribbon shirts and dresses. The pottery often features a red clay with portions covered with a cream-colored slip that is painted with simple geometric designs, abstract clouds, flowers, and turkey eyes. Perhaps the pueblo's best-known artist is Art Menchengo, who works in watercolors, oil paints, and various drawing media, including charcoal.

VISITING SANTA ANA

DIRECTIONS: Located 16 miles north of **Albuquerque**. To get to the tourism facilities, head north from **Albuquerque** on I-25. Take Exit 242 at **Bernalillo** and proceed 2.5 miles west on NM 44 to Tamaya Boulevard (opposite NM 528). The historic village is open to the public occasionally. To reach it, continue west on NM 44 for another 8 miles. Watch for the historic plaque and sign on the right marking the village access road.

VISITOR CENTER/MUSEUM: **Tamaya Cultural Center**, located in the **Hyatt Regency** hotel (open daily 9 A.M.-5 P.M.), presents the history, culture, and art of the Santa Ana people.

PHOTOGRAPHY: Permission required from the Governor's Office.

SKETCHING/SOUND RECORDING: Not allowed.

CASINO: **Santa Ana Star Casino** offers blackjack, poker, slot machines, craps, roulette, mini-baccarat, and slots, and **Canyon Lounge** presents nightly live entertainment. The complex will also have a thirty-six-lane bowling center, a 3,000-seat special events center, and conference space. (505) 867-0000.

DINING: **Prairie Star Restaurant** is a top-notch dining establishment popular with Albuquerque diners who appreciate fine cuisine and outstanding views of the Rio Grande Valley and Sandia Mountains. The attractive facility is housed in an adobe home, originally built in 1920, and features exposed viga-and-latilla ceilings and numerous fireplaces. A patio provides wonderful outdoor dining in warm weather. Specialties include bison ribeye, poblano chiles stuffed with shrimp, and Chama Valley lamb chops. There is an extensive wine selection. Located north of the casino, just off Tamaya Boulevard/Jemez Canyon Dam Road. (505) 867-3327. Open Tues.–Sun. 5:30–9 P.M.

Wind Dancer Bar & Grill, which adjoins the **Prairie Star Restaurant**, serves hearty breakfasts, lunch fare, and afternoon appetizers. (505) 867-9190. Open daily year round, except in extreme winter weather, 7:30 A.M.–6 P.M.

Santa Ana Star Casino offers four places to eat, including a buffet-style restaurant open for breakfast, lunch, and dinner; and a fine-dining establishment.

Hyatt Regency Resort offers fine dining at **Corn Maiden**, and more casual service at **Santa Ana Cafe**, **Ahtosh Bar and Grill**, **Cottonwood Lounge**, and the **Spa Cafe and Juice Bar**. Poolside service also is available.

ACCOMMODATIONS: Attractive and comfortable, the **Hyatt Regency Tamaya Resort & Spa** may well be the nation's foremost Indian-based resort. The facility, a partnership between the Hyatt Corporation and Santa Ana Pueblo, includes 350 guest rooms and suites, five restaurants and lounges, business meeting facilities, a championship eighteen-hole golf course, a 16,000-square-foot spa and fitness center, three outdoor heated pools (one with water slides, sprays, and other activity features), a salon, gift shop and deli, culture center, and tennis courts. The resort also offers a children's program, horseback riding, and a nature trail along the Rio Grande. (505) 867-1234 or (800) 55-HYATT.

To reach the **Hyatt**, drive to the **Santa Ana Star Casino** and proceed north on Tamaya Boulevard to Tuyuna Trail and follow the signs. The new **Santa Ana Star Casino Hotel** nearby offers 288 guest rooms.

CAMPING: Camping is not permitted.

RECREATION: The twenty-seven-hole **Santa Ana Golf Course** is a highly regarded facility overlooking the Rio Grande Valley. Facilities include a large clubhouse, pro shop, and practice area. Guests of the **Hyatt Regency** can also play on the eighteen-hole **Twin Warriors Championship Course** designed by Gary Parks. (505) 867-9464, www.santaanagolf.com.

Even most Albuquerque residents may not be aware of another Santa Ana attraction, **Jemez Canyon**. The Army Corps of Engineers erected a flood control dam here in 1950 that created a small reservoir beneath black-lipped mesas. The reservoir is off-limits for recreation, but a picnic area overlooks the lake and the **Rio Grande Valley** to the east. To get here, travel north from the **Santa Ana Star Casino** 6.5 miles on the old Jemez Dam Road, an extension of Tamaya Boulevard. The site contains six ramadas with picnic tables, and portable toilets are nearby. Entry is free.

The Santa Ana tribe also owns and manages a **hunting** and **fishing** ranch in the south-central part of the state, near Riudoso, called **Bonney Canyon Ranch**. For details, call (505) 867-4206.

ARTISTS AND GALLERIES: A handful of Santa Ana women maintain the **Ta-Ma-Ya Crafts Cooperative**, which opened in the 1980s. Here you can find traditional embroidered cloth and clothing, redware painted with clay pigments and other natural materials, silver and turquoise jewelry, Pueblo-style woven belts, and ceremonial ribbon shirts and dresses. Located at 2 Dove Rd., next to the tribal library, in the village of **Los Ranchos**. Open in summer, Tues. and Thurs. 10 A.M.–4 P.M. Cash and checks only.

Art Menchengo is an artist whose favorite subject matter is Native American portraits. He also renders animals and some landscapes in watercolors, oil paints, and various drawing media, including charcoal. P.O. Box 68, Bernalillo, NM 87004. (505) 867-4485. Open year round, but call first for directions.

The tribe owns and operates **Warrior Apparel**, which features reproductions of Indian art on T-shirts, sweatshirts, denim jackets, bags, and other textile products. In addition to Art Menchengo, Warrior Apparel also relies on the graphic talents of Sioux, Navajo, Hopi, and Kiowa artists. Located next to the casino. (800) 867-4260.

The **Prairie Star Gift Shop**, located inside the casino, carries a limited selection of pottery produced in various pueblos, some Indian CDs and books, and Warrior Apparel T-shirts.

SANTA CLARA

(SAHN-ta KLAH-rah)

Kha P'o: "Valley of Wild Roses"
Ka-poo: "Singing Water"

SANTA CLARA IS ONE of the most popular pueblos for visitors, and for good reason. Its tribal members are among the most artistically active of all the pueblos, and fine works by Santa Clara artists can be found in a large number of shops and studios in the village. Tourists are encouraged to wander the village, visit the shops, and meet the artists at work. Even guided tours are offered, some of which include full meals.

Also located within the reservation is one of the Southwest's most impressive, publicly accessible prehistoric ruins—the Puye Cliff Dwellings, a National Historic Landmark. While many pueblos lost their mountain lands over the centuries, Santa Clara retained some high country holdings in the breathtakingly beautiful Jemez Mountains to the west of the village.

History

Santa Clara ancestors most likely migrated south from the Four Corners region to the Chama River Valley, eventually reaching the Pajarito Plateau on the eastern slope of the Jemez Mountains between A.D. 1100 and 1300.

Here these Tewa-speaking people established several pueblos, including Puye. The pueblo's first rooms were simply dug into the relatively soft tuff, or compacted volcanic ash, of the canyon walls. Later, additional rooms were built out from the cliff face and atop the mesa with cut tuff blocks. By 1400 as many as fifteen hundred people occupied

up to one thousand rooms. A major drought forced the inhabitants to abandon Puye in the sixteenth century. The people moved down canyon to a more reliable water source, the Rio Grande, and established the current village on the west bank.

Here along the river they farmed corn, squash, melons, and other crops, and supplemented their diet with buffalo meat from the Great Plains to the east; deer, turkey, antelope, and elk found in the surrounding mountains and foothills; and fish from the Rio Grande.

In 1598, Spanish colonists from nearby Yunque (today's San Juan Pueblo) brought Franciscan missionaries to Santa Clara, and a Catholic church was erected circa 1622. The people of Santa Clara, like those of the other pueblos, resented the Spanish intrusion and the theft of their food and land, and actively participated in the Pueblo Revolt of 1680. One of the prominent leaders of the revolt was a Santa Clara man named Domingo Naranjo, who was of mixed black and Pueblo heritage.

The Spanish returned in 1692, and the pueblo was temporarily abandoned in 1696. Even after the people returned to Santa Clara in the eighteenth century, disease, including smallpox, took its toll on the population. This trend continued even into the twentieth century, when an epidemic of Spanish flu after World War I swept through the pueblo.

right: Redware pot
by Jody Powell, Santa Clara
STEPHEN TRIMBLE

Contemporary Life

Today, Santa Clara is home to about twenty-six hundred people. Many work at the Los Alamos National Laboratories, in adjoining Española, or in Santa Fe, but a sizeable percentage are artists or craftspeople. The tribe's 47,000 acres still support some farming along the valley floor, and the surrounding foothills and mountains provide forage for livestock.

Santa Clara Canyon, a major drainage, flows eastward off the shoulders of the highest massif in the Jemez Mountains, 11,561-foot-high Santa Clara (Tschicoma) Peak. The tribe once operated a large campground here with several placid fishing lakes formed by beaver dams. Lush pine and aspen forests flanked grassy meadows dotted with wildflowers, while far below spread the tan and pink hills and flats of the Rio Grande Valley. This recreation area was closed to the public in the wake the devastating Los Alamos wildfire in 2000, but the tribe hopes to reopen it when conditions permit.

A small casino and bowling center, which the tribe opened in Española in 2001, should help fund additional tribal endeavors in the future.

Art, Crafts, and Culture

Santa Clara is best known as a center for magnificent pottery, and perhaps as many as one in four residents is a potter. The pueblo is home to many artistic dynasties. One of the most famous is the Tafoya clan, led by Margaret Tafoya (1904-2001). The clan also includes her sister Tomasita Naranjo (1884-1918), Tomasita's daughter Nicholasa and her granddaughter Roberta Naranjo; and Margaret's other sisters, Christina Naranjo (1891-1980) and Camilio Sunflower (1902-1995). Following in Sunflower's footsteps are Lucy "Year Flower" Tafoya, Grace Medicine Flower, Joseph Lonewolf, his son Gregory Lonewolf, and his daughters Susan "Snowflake" Romero and Rosemary Lonewolf. Many of Tafoya's own children have become potters, as well. These include Lu Ann Tafoya, Mela Youngblood and her children Nathan and Nancy Youngblood-Lugo, and Toni Roller. Roller's offspring involved in pottery include children and grandchildren, such as Cliff Roller, Jeff Roller, Susan Roller Whittington and Charles Lewis.

Santa Clara is best known for the lustrous blackware and redware its many artists produce. The artisans employ these clays in a profusion of forms, including vases, bowls, and figurines. The black and redware are both made from the same base clay, dug by hand on the reservation. The blackware receives its characteristic coloration in the firing process when the fire is smothered with piles of manure. The porous clay absorbs the carbon in the smoke.

Another defining characteristic of Santa Clara's pottery is the widespread use of deep carving, which is done after the clay has dried to a leathery consistency.

Nancy Youngblood-Lugo is one of the pueblo's best-known potters. She creates works of superb proportion and finish. She is particularly well known for creating melon bowls, round vessels with heavy ridges radiating outward in a spiral like an acorn squash. Her success has led many other potters to revive this once-obscure form.

Ron Suazo, Grace Medicine Flower, and Joseph Lonewolf work in a shallower, finer sgraffito carving style. In this process, a sharp blade or point is used to scratch away a surface design after the piece has been fired, to create finely detailed designs of animals and geometric motifs. Jody Powell is another masterful Santa Clara potter who often works in the finer, etching style with nontraditional design elements, including Northwest Coastal Native motifs. Her pieces tend to be four to six inches in height.

While pottery is the traditional art form for which Santa Clara is best known, resident artisans also work in embroidery, beadwork, weaving, and woodcarving. A handful of others work in other media, as well; internationally renowned sculptor Roxanne Swentzell, for example, works in stone and bronze to create captivating character studies of Pueblo subjects.

Nora Naranjo Morse is another Santa Clara woman working in novel media, including sculpture, installation pieces, and video production.

Michael Naranjo, who was blinded in Vietnam, is a talented bronze and stone sculptor. He has received several national sculpture commissions, including a large work for the Veterans

Administration Building in Washington, D.C.

Pablita Velarde of Santa Clara was one of the first Pueblo artists to gain international renown with her detailed paintings and murals of traditional Pueblo scenes, which she first began creating at the Santa Fe Indian School under Dorothy Dunn in the 1930s. Traditionalists did not appreciate her fame, and she has not resided at the pueblo since her school days. Her late daughter, Helen Hardin, was also a well-regarded, gifted artist who was a painter and printmaker.

The pueblo's original Catholic church was destroyed in the Pueblo Revolt, and two subsequent structures also fell. The current adobe building, with its low bell tower and turquoise doors and lintels, was erected in 1918. Note that visitors are not allowed to enter the cemetery.

Pottery burners, Santa Clara, 1905
Edward S. Curtis

Visiting Santa Clara

DIRECTIONS: From **Santa Fe**, take US 84/285 for 24 miles to **Española**, crossing to the west bank of the **Rio Grande**. Turn south (left) onto NM 30 and proceed to the first village entrance road on the left. The Governor's Office ("Neighborhood Facility") is straight ahead a half mile on the right. The church and plaza are both a bit farther along this road, on the south side of the Santa Clara creek bed, which is often dry. An alternative, more scenic route from **Santa Fe** takes you north on US 84/285 to NM 502 past **San Ildefonso Pueblo** to the west bank of the **Rio Grande**, and then north on NM 30 to the village entrance.

TOURS: **Ancient Storytelling Learning Center** can organize custom outings that might include a pottery-making demonstration, visits to artist studios, a general tour of the village or the **Puye Cliff Dwellings**, dancing, and a traditional feast in a tribal member's home. Costs depend on the nature of the tour. **Singing Water Gallery** also conducts guided tours. Cost per person is $12.50 for the two-hour **Puye Cliff Dwellings** tour, $10 for the one-hour village tour, and $18 for a three-hour combination tour. (505) 753-6901 or (505) 852-2650. PO Box 1979, Espanola, NM 87532.

PHOTOGRAPHY: A $5, one-day still camera permit may be obtained from the Governor's Office. A video permit costs $15.

SKETCHING/SOUND RECORDING: A permit for sketching, also available from the Governor's Office, costs $25 a day. Sound recording is not allowed.

CASINO: The tribe operates a casino in **Española**, on Riverside Drive on the north side of town, with slots, blackjack, craps, a twenty-four-lane bowling center, and restaurant.

DINING: Hot food can be purchased from **street vendors** at major public events. The adjoining town of **Española** also has many dining options, including local favorite **Paragua**.

RECREATION: **Puye Cliff Dwellings** are located above the village in a canyon of the **Pajarito Plateau**. Three hiking trails lead across the canyon floor, up to the cliff base, and up a series of ladders to the mesa top, where the ruins of what was once a four-story stone pueblo are located.

Guided tours are available daily from late April through September (except June 13 and Aug. 12), and the site is open daily year round for self-guided tours (except as noted above and during winter storms). Summer hours run 8 A.M.–8 P.M.; and otherwise 8 A.M.–4 P.M. Admission is $5 per person. Proceed south on NM 30 and look for the turnoff at Mile Marker 5 onto Forest Service Road 602. The cliff dwellings are seven miles up the well-maintained gravel road.

ARTISTS AND GALLERIES: **Merrock Galleria** presents pottery, paintings, lithographs, and bronze sculptures by owner **Paul Speckled Rock**. The shop also carries Navajo, Hopi, and Santo Domingo silver and turquoise jewelry, typical carved red and black pottery by various potters, and pottery from other pueblos. Also available are Pueblo willow baskets. Paul's wife, **Rosalda**, contributes paintings—in oil, watercolor and acrylics—and beadwork, including miniature beaded bags. Located on the northwest corner of the plaza. (505) 753-2083. Open daily, 9:30 A.M.–5:30 P.M. Visa and MasterCard accepted.

Naranjo Pottery carries a selection of blackware, including works by **Sammy Naranjo**, who creates vessels featuring black bases and red tops, which are then etched. The shop also carries miniature pottery by **Candelario Suazo** and **Barbara Martinez**, beaded necklaces from Santo Domingo, and handmade drums by **Gilbert Herrera** of Cochiti. Located on the south side of the plaza. (505) 747-9035. Open in summer, 9 A.M.–6 P.M., otherwise 11 A.M.–4 P.M.

Madeline Naranjo and daughter **Frances** produce deep-carved blackware wedding vases, turtle figurines, and miniatures. Located on the south side of the village. (505) 753-8315. Open daily, but call first.

Corn's Studio features the pottery of **Corn Moquino** and his family, including carved blackware vases and bowls (some with lids), and animal figurines, including hummingbirds, unusual open-mouthed fish, and turtles. He occasionally adorns his vessels with turquoise. The shop also has a selection of gourd rattles and jewelry. Located on the north side of the village. Open daily in summer, 10 A.M.–6 P.M., otherwise 10 A.M.–4 P.M. Major charge cards accepted.

Singing Water Gallery owners **Joe** and **Nora Baca** specialize in pottery by leading artists, including **Joseph Lonewolf**, **Kevin Naranjo**, **Doles** and **Alvin Curran**, **Madeline Naranjo**, **Angela David**, and **Alvin Baca**. The gallery also carries jewelry, Zuni fetishes, and paintings and drawings. (505) 753-9663 or (888) 430-6222. Open year round, Mon.–Sat. 10 A.M.–5:30 P.M., except major holidays. Major credit cards accepted.

Toni Roller's Studio and Gallery features traditional, deep-carved blackware. **Jeff Roller** also makes lovely, chocolate brown slip-covered jars capped by sculpted buffalo lids. **Shirley Tafoya** produces unusual coiled miniatures, most of which are usually teased from pinch pots. Located on the west side of NM 30, just south of the main entrance to the village. (505) 753-3003. Open year round, Mon.–Sat. 10 A.M.–5 P.M. Visa and MasterCard accepted.

Ron Suazo Studio features inlaid turquoise, lapis and other stones, carved and incised surfaces, polished black on matte and sienna surfaces, and elaborate lids. (505) 753-5260 or www.newmexico.com/santaclarapottery. Open year round, Mon.–Fri. 10 A.M.–5 P.M. and Sat. 1–5 P.M.

Anita Suazo Studio presents pottery of this award-winning artist, including red-carved, red polychrome, black-carved and black-on-black vessels using locally gathered clay, hand-building, and traditional firing processes. P.O. Box 389, Española, NM 87532. (505) 753-2724.

Michael Tsosie Sisneros Studio highlights the fine mask-like paintings and works on paper of this award-winning artist of Navajo/Santa Clara/Laguna/Mission Indian heritage. He also is a noted apparel designer. P.O. Box 873, Espanola, NM 87532.

Tina Garcia is yet another notable Santa Clara potter who works in finely rendered traditional forms. (505) 753-1764.

SANTO DOMINGO

(SAHN-toh doh-MEEN-go)

Indian name uncertain

Santo Domingo, 1925
T. HARMON PARKHURST

ONE OF THE MOST POPULOUS yet least open of all New Mexico pueblos, Santo Domingo is home to many talented artists who rely on contact with outside markets for their livelihood and are happy to see visitors.

The tribal government's reluctance to promote visitation may be attributable to the fact that Santa Domingo residents historically have been among the most active of pueblo traders. The prevailing philosophy seems to be "Don't come to us; we'll come to you."

Still, those who venture to Santo Domingo will discover an especially lovely Catholic church and a handful of fine arts and crafts shops. Its annual August corn dance is the largest such event open to the public among the nineteen pueblos,

and its Labor Day weekend arts and crafts fair is a fine occasion at which to peruse the work of hundreds of artists.

History

Like its neighbors Cochiti and San Felipe, Santo Domingo is a Keres-speaking pueblo established in the fifteenth century by immigrants from villages atop the nearby Pajarito Plateau. Alonzo Catiti led Santo Domingo and the other Keres pueblos in the Pueblo Revolt of 1680. Catiti and Popé of San Juan apparently held a feast at Santa Ana Pueblo to celebrate their victory, and drank from communion chalices from the churches while cursing the Catholic priests.

Spanish Governor Antonio Otermin, on a reprisal mission of 1681, found Santo Domingo unoccupied. Residents had fled to a nearby mesa-top stronghold for safety. Otermin burned the pueblo. In 1692, the returning Spanish under Diego de Vargas stormed the mountain refuge, and burned it as well. Catiti died in this battle and Keres opposition to the Spanish crumbled. Most survivors fled, some to Acoma, but over time many drifted back. Around 1793 refugees from the pueblos of the Galisteo River drainage, ravaged by nomadic raiders and disease, moved into Santo Domingo. The pueblo's current village was apparently occupied about 1886.

Santo Domingo was the site in 1598 of the first gathering of thirty-eight pueblo governors when Spanish Governor Don Juan de Oñate called on the Pueblo peoples to pledge allegiance to the Spanish Crown. Today the All Indian Pueblo Council (consisting of the nineteen pueblo governors and an executive staff) assembles here for its first meeting of the year, continuing this oldest of America's political gatherings. The pueblo also served as the headquarters for the Franciscan missionaries in New Mexico. It was the seat of church records, and during the Spanish Inquisition, religious trials were held here.

VISITING SANTO DOMINGO

DIRECTIONS: Located midway between **Albuquerque** and **Santa Fe**. Take I-25 north from **Albuquerque** or south from **Santa Fe** 30 miles. Take Exit 259 and proceed west on NM 22 into the **Rio Grande Valley**. Cross over the railroad bridge, circle under it (Caution trailers: The bridge clearance is only 13'10"), and continue another mile or so west into the village center.

VISITOR CENTER/MUSEUM: None.

TOURS: None.

PHOTOGRAPHY: Not allowed.

SKETCHING/SOUND RECORDING: Not allowed.

DINING: No restaurants, but a few families sell snacks and sandwiches.

ACCOMMODATIONS: None. Many hotel rooms are available in **Albuquerque** and **Santa Fe**.

CAMPING: Not permitted.

RECREATION: Not available.

ARTISTS AND GALLERIES: Santo Domingo is home to lots of artists and craftspeople. Many maintain small shops clustered around the large entry plaza surrounding the church, and along the village access road.

Joe V. Tortalita has been producing silver jewelry, heishi, and turquoise beads for more than thirty-five years "from raw on up," as he puts it. Located north of the church. Look for his sign. Call first, (505) 465-2973.

Rosetta's Trading Post carries sandwiches, snack items, pop, and occasionally horno-baked bread, as well as a bit of jewelry. Located on the west side of the main plaza. (505) 465-2504. Open daily.

Dan's Trading Post is a small general store with an interesting assortment of arts and crafts, including Navajo rugs; jewelry from Hopi, Navajo, Zuni and Santo Domingo; Plains Indian beadwork; and general antiques. Located on the east side of the entry plaza. Open daily 9 A.M. to sunset. Closed during ceremonies.

Ginny's Food and Pottery Shop carries pottery and jewelry made by the **Genevieve** and **Joseph Garcia** family. You can also chow down on Frito pies, fry bread, Indian tacos, and traditional horno-baked bread. Located on the village access road. (505) 465-0425. Open daily.

Ca Win, also known as **Jimmy F. Calbaza**, produces outstanding heishi, often strung on fine necklaces. He also works with large stones in rings, bracelets, and other forms. He is also a good farmer, cultivating more than one hundred acres of chile, corn, and other foods. His studio is located off the main access road, on the west side of main plaza. Follow the signs. Open Sept.–Jan. Call first, (505) 465-2832.

Lorenzo and **Stephanie Garcia** are rarities: Pueblo weavers who produce finely woven mantas (shawls) and kilts in traditional Pueblo style. P.O. Box 512, Santo Domingo, NM 87052. (505) 867-4036.

Chavez Creations, owned by **Joe** and **Lejeune Chavez**, is the most diverse of Santo Domingo shops. It carries several

pottery styles, including a black-on-black ware made by a family relative, **Olivia Coriz**; and a black-and-brown-on-orange ware with birds and flower designs. **Joe** produces silver overlay jewelry, and **Lejeune** contemporary beadwork. Manufactured goods, including Pendleton blankets and shawls, moccasins, handbags, silk scarves, and T-shirts are also for sale. Located on the village access road. Call first. (505) 867-1777.

The **Chavez** family also run a larger store called **Pueblo House** at the **!Traditions! Marketplace**. The shop has a large selection of beaded goods (including fine Shoshone work) and jewelry, as well as handmade drums by Santo Domingoan **Irvin Coriz** and beaded moccasins from various Plains tribes. It also has an interesting assortment of reproduced artifacts of various tribes. Located on I-25, Exit 257. (505) 867-1777. Open year round, Mon.–Sat. 10 A.M.–6 P.M., Sun. 11 A.M.–6 P.M. Major credit cards accepted.

Henry Rosetta produces a variety of fine jewelry of stone and shell set in sterling silver and gold. One of the first artisans to popularize the "chiclets" style (corn kernel-sized raw stones strung on a necklace), this award-winning artist is also the inventor of a unique pendant form that allows the wearer to slip five different stone inlay inserts in and out of a hand-shaped silver setting depending on your mood. He also produces handmade heishi (a Santo Domingo specialty), dangling earrings, bolos, rings, and knives. Located at **Santo Domingo Station**, several miles from the village. Open daily, but call first, (505) 465-0722.

Contemporary Life

The tribe has a population of more than forty-five hundred people, two-thirds of whom live on the reservation. Many tribal members work in Albuquerque, but some of the farm fields and orchards on the valley floor are still productive. Altogether, the reservation encompasses 81,000 acres, including upland mesas, grasslands, a portion of the Galisteo Creek drainage, and a stretch of the Rio Grande.

Art, Crafts, and Culture

In addition to their historic role as traders, the people of Santo Domingo were known as the best of the Pueblo beadmakers. A word often used for Pueblo tubular-style beads in general, heishi, comes from a Keres word meaning "shell." Shell was a popular material used to produce beads in the past, and still is. The pueblo's skilled heishi makers also work with a wide variety of stone and other base materials. The base material is first cut into small squares, then a tiny hole is drilled through the center and it is strung. Next comes lengthy grinding and polishing steps as the bead is rounded and smoothed. The labor-intensive work is a specialty of Santo Domingo artisans, with a handful still working the old way.

The pueblo is home to many jewelers who work with turquoise and a wide variety of other materials. In prehistoric times, Santo Domingo people actively mined turquoise from an area now known as the Turquoise Hills, and traded it as far south as central Mexico. Pueblo artisans are still noted for their work in "chunk style" (and the smaller "chiclets" style) of jewelry. Santo Domingo jewelers also often work in mosaic inlay, in which cut stones are laid over a backing. Notable jewelers include Angie Reano Owen, Martine Lovato, and Jessie and Paul Rosetta. Gail Bird, of Laguna/Santo Domingo heritage, is one of the most renowned of all Pueblo jewelry designers, but her work is not found on the reservation.

Santo Domingo also is noted for its pottery, which is often blocky with bold geometric patterns,

because the use of sacred symbols and animal imagery, except birds, is frowned on. Potter Robert Tenorio often creates large bowls decorated with handsome, geometric black and dull red designs. Potters Paulita and Gilbert Pacheco work in large vessels with black-and-white geometric designs on an orangish base, and black animal figures on a creamy white base.

The Santo Domingo church also makes a memorable impression. The mission-style adobe has a white exterior, and over its entry doors hangs a bell above a wooden balcony.

Santo Domingo once had a train station where Pueblo artists would sell their goods to travelers passing through. The train no longer stops here, and the station—with its colorful, tourist-attracting facade—was destroyed by fire in 2001.

SANTO DOMINGO

Must-see: Santo Domingo church, artist shops

January 1: dances

Easter Sunday: Catholic mass at midnight the evening prior, with dances during the day

August 4: Santo Domingo Feast Day, with massive corn dances, many food and arts and crafts booths, even an occasional traveling carnival

Labor Day weekend: arts and crafts fair with more than three hundred artisans, food booths, and dancing, held at Exit 259 on I-25

P.O. Box 99,
Santo Domingo Pueblo, NM 87052
Governor's Office, (505) 465-2214

TAOS

(TAH-ose)

Tuah-Tah: "Our Village" or "At Red Willow Canyon Mouth"

THE HISTORIC MULTISTORIED VILLAGE of Taos Pueblo is the most photographed site among New Mexico's nineteen pueblos. The adobe structure, which rises as high as five stories, is a National Historic Landmark and was designated as a World Heritage Site by the United Nations in 1992. To preserve the essential character of the pueblo, which appears today much as it did in the seventeenth century when the Spanish arrived, there is neither electricity nor indoor plumbing.

Behind the village, to the east, rise the tallest peaks of the Sangre de Cristo Mountains, including imposing Taos Mountain. The Rio Pueblo, which the people of Taos call Red Willow, flows from its source—sacred Blue Lake—high in the pine-forested Sangre de Cristo range and bisects the village, carrying its life-giving waters to fields and pastures.

Only about fifty people live fulltime in the historic village today. Most Taos residents live outside the old village in modern homes but maintain family residences within the old district, where they honor their ancestors by performing the sacred ceremonies. San Geronimo Feast Day at Taos is one of the most popular of all Pueblo gatherings and attracts native and non-native visitors.

Taos Pueblo is home to numerous artists and craftspeople, and among all pueblos has the greatest number of shops open to visitors. The pueblo attracts more visitors than any other and exerts a powerful presence over the sage mesa country of the Upper Rio Grande Valley.

Replastering Taos Pueblo
STEPHEN TRIMBLE

History

The two main structures of the historic pueblo are the large room blocks called Hlaauma (North House) and Hlaukkwima (South House), both located on the banks of the Rio Pueblo. These complexes are believed to be more than a thousand years old, which would make Taos one of the oldest continually inhabited sites in North America, along with Sky City at Acoma Pueblo and the Hopi village of Old Orabi in Arizona.

Historically, residents lived in the upper and outer rooms, while the chambers deep within the pueblo were used to store food and other materials. In the days of armed conflict with nomadic tribes and the Spanish, ground-floor rooms were not accessible through doorways. Residents entered rooms through ceiling holes. Ladders were required to reach the roofs and to enter each room, and these ladders could be removed to deny attackers

Christmas eve luminarias, Taos
STEPHEN TRIMBLE

access. As another defensive measure, outside rooms did not have windows. The doors and windows that appear today on the exterior room walls of the historic pueblos are a modern adaptation.

A 10-foot-high wall with five watchtowers once surrounded the historic village. Only low sections of this wall remain, as a de-facto boundary between the "old" world and the new.

Taos Pueblo has played a prominent role in many of New Mexico's most important historic events. The leader of the Pueblo Revolt of 1680, Popé of San Juan, hid at Taos while finalizing plans for the uprising, and Taos Pueblo warriors took part in the revolt.

As the northernmost pueblo, Taos is close to the principal mountain pass linking the pueblo world with the Great Plains and thus it had greater contact with Plains Indian cultures than most other pueblos. Usually the Apaches, Comanches, and other nomadic people of the Plains came in peace to trade. Taos residents would trade pottery vessels, blankets, foods and other goods in exchange for buffalo meat and hides, and other goods that the nomadic tribes offered. Over time, the pueblo developed a flourishing trade that grew to include the Spanish, then the Mexicans, and finally the mountain men of the early American period.

In 1847, following the American occupation of New Mexico, some disaffected Spanish-speaking residents of the area and elements of Taos Pueblo joined forces in a disastrous revolt against "Los Americanos." They attacked the home of U.S. Territorial Governor Charles Bent in the town of Taos and killed and beheaded him. His wife and family escaped by digging through an adobe wall into an adjoining home. The U.S. Army counter-attacked, torching the pueblo's original San Geronimo church in which they believed the rebels were holed up. Tragically, only innocent women, children, and old men had sought refuge in the church, and all perished. The action nevertheless ended the short-lived rebellion, and today a crumbling bell tower is all that remains of the mission chapel, which was built in 1619.

Visiting Taos

DIRECTIONS: Located on the northern edge of the town of **Taos**, 65 miles north of **Santa Fe**. From the town of **Taos**, head north on Paseo del Pueblo Norte (the main north-south road though town). Just past the **Kachina Lodge**, bear right at the Y and proceed 2 miles north to the parking area just outside the historic village core.

VISITOR INFORMATION: The pueblo is open to visitors Mon.–Sat. 8 A.M.–5 P.M., and Sun. 8:30 A.M.–5 P.M. It is closed to the public from mid-February to early April. Restrooms are located at the entrance to the historic village. Entrance fee is $10 per adult or $8 per person for groups of five or more, $8 for seniors, $3 for students ages thirteen to eighteen.

TOURS: The **Taos Pueblo Tourism Department** can organize guided tours from April through early November for individuals or groups. Advance reservations are suggested. **Student guides** also conduct group tours daily on a gratuity basis. Details are available at the information and fee booth at the entrance to the historic village.

PHOTOGRAPHY: Commercial photography requires special written permission and fees. Personal camera permits are $10 per day. Video camera permits are $20 a day. Visitors are forbidden from photographing ceremonies (except for the annual Taos Pueblo Pow Wow), the kivas, and the church interior. Photos of people require their consent.

SKETCHING/SOUND RECORDING: Permission to sketch must be obtained in advance. Sound recording is not allowed.

CASINO: **Taos Mountain Casino** offers blackjack, slots, roulette, and video poker. Free shuttle service runs from various locations in the town of **Taos**. Located on the main road into the historic village. (888) WIN-TAOS or (505) 737-0777. Open Sun.–Thurs., 8 A.M.–2 P.M.; Fri.–Sat., 8 A.M.–3 P.M.

DINING: For a sit-down meal, try **Tiwa Kitchen**, one of the few Pueblo-style restaurants serving modestly priced, tasty traditional fare, including Pueblo stew, buffalo burgers, stuffed fry bread, grilled buffalo and onions over wild rice,

and trout. **Tiwa Kitchen** also serves New Mexican fare such as green chile stew, enchiladas, and burritos. For dessert, there's chocolate squash cake or prune pie. Owners and Taos residents **Ben White Buffalo** and **Debbie Moonlight Flowers** add a homey warmth with a corner fireplace and music. The restaurant also carries a small but enticing selection of canned and dried foodstuffs, including blue corn mix, Pueblo red chile, and chokecherry jam. Dinners, group meals, and catering can be arranged with advance notice. Located just outside the historic village core on Taos Pueblo Road. (505) 751-1020. Open Wed.–Mon., Apr.–Oct. 11 A.M.–7 P.M.; Nov.–Mar. 11 A.M.–5 P.M. Visa and MasterCard accepted.

The Lucky 7 Cafe serves breakfast, lunch, and dinner. Located in **Taos Mountain Casino**. Open Sun.–Thurs. 10 A.M.–10 P.M. and Fri.–Sat. 10 A.M.–midnight.

ACCOMMODATIONS: The town of **Taos** and surrounding area contains scores of hotels, lodges, motels, bed-and-breakfasts, and commercial campgrounds.

CAMPING: Not allowed, including the lands within the **Blue Lake Wilderness Area**. There are many public campgrounds in nearby **Carson National Forest**.

RECREATION: Activities outside the historic village are forbidden. However, you can see more of the reservation by visiting the **Taos Indian Horse Ranch**, which offers one- and two-hour rides ($85–$110 per person) to overnight outings. It operates year round, weather permitting, with about forty horses ranging from kid-friendly plodders to speedy steeds for expert riders. The **Besario "Storm Star" Gomez** family has run this operation since 1968. Call for directions. (505) 758-3212, (800) 659-3210, or hoofbeats@laplaza.org.

ARTISTS AND GALLERIES: Taos Pueblo has a plethora of shops and artist studios. These include two excellent galleries–perhaps the best of all those among the nineteen pueblos.

Tony Reyna Indian Shop is a fascinating gallery. Opened in 1950 by former pueblo governor **Tony Reyna**, it is packed with fine arts and crafts by

Taos artisans, as well as work by artists from many other pueblos, and a few Plains Indian artisans. Works by Taos artists include micaceous clay fetishes by **Darlene Track**, and drums, silver jewelry, paintings, bronzes, pastels, and monoprints by **Diane Reyna**. There are examples of fine Hopi, Navajo, and Zuni jewelry; large stone sculptures; pipes; Christmas tree ornaments; prints, paintings and posters; and pottery from San Juan, Acoma, Santa Clara, and Santo Domingo. Collectors will enjoy the pottery dating from the 1930s. Other historic pots, baskets, and photos add to the ambience. Located on Taos Pueblo Road. (505) 758-3835. Open 8 A.M.–5 P.M. in summer, 8:30–4 P.M. fall through spring, except major holidays.

Behind an unpretentious exterior at **Wahleah's Taos Pueblo Gallery** lies a delightful series of five display rooms filled with art, crafts, and clothing. **Lucinda** and **Pete Bernal** set up shop in the 1930s to sell moccasins, beadwork, and pottery. Their granddaughter, **Wahleah**, operates the gallery today with family and friends. **Wahleah** strives to carry high-quality pottery from all nineteen pueblos, as well as the Hopi and Navajo nations. Features are works by renowned artists, including traditional micaceous work by the likes of Taos potter **Michael Marcus**. Also displayed are stone sculptures by **Louis** and **Ned Archuleta** (no relation), immense, table-sized deerskin drums by **Dean Lujan** of Taos, Navajo rugs, and katsina dolls. The exceptional gallery is located within the historic village core, on the south side of the stream. (505) 758-9765. Open 8:30 A.M.–5 P.M. in summer, 9 A.M.–4 P.M. fall through spring. Major credit cards accepted.

Around the large plaza within the historic village core are dozens of small shops and studio galleries. Most, but not all, accept credit cards.

Evening Snow Comes Gallery focuses on the award-winning visual art of **David Gary Suazo**, his wife **Geraldine Tso**, and their children. Opened in 1991, the gallery displays paintings in acrylics, oil pastels, and watercolors on handmade paper, as well as quilts by **Geraldine Tso**. Located at the entrance to the historic village. (505) 751-0591. Usually open fall through winter when the artists are not otherwise on the road.

(continues on next page)

Contemporary Life

In the twentieth century, the people of Taos Pueblo have waged a different sort of struggle, this one to reclaim tribal ownership of sacred Blue Lake. Though historically within the pueblo's sphere of influence, the lake was considered by the government to be on federal land, and in 1906 officially became part of Carson National Forest. While non-natives were permitted to graze cattle and camp on its shores, the people of Taos were not able to hold important ceremonies there. After a decades-long struggle, the tribe prevailed, and in 1970 President Nixon signed legislation that returned the lake and surrounding area to the pueblo's control.

Today Taos Pueblo controls a land base of approximately 105,000 acres, and has a population of about twenty-two hundred tribal members, a fairly large number of whom are artists. Some residents still farm, but most adults work off the reservation in the town of Taos and beyond. With their strong community support system, residents have a safety net of sorts, rich in tradition and values. They are pleased to be living at the foot of the big mountain in the place where the stream runs out through the red willows and cottonwood groves.

Art, Crafts, and Culture

Many pueblo residents make a living as artists, working in an unusually broad range of media. The majority of Taos artists are potters, including those who produce storyteller dolls and those who create the pueblo's popular lidded, micaceous bean pots.

Taos also is home to numerous jewelers; some of the finest Pueblo leather crafters, including drummaker Lee Lujan and moccasin makers Luke and Mildred Young; stone sculptor Ned Archuleta; flute

VISITING TAOS

(continued from page 81)

Mirabal Pottery Shop features the work of **Tony Mirabal**, mostly pottery, some with an unusual horsehair finish, and etched and polished seed pots. His unique five-hole ocarinas (clay flutes) create wonderful music. He also has a small selection of jewelry. Located at the entrance to the historic village, next to the church. (505) 758-1740. mirabalspottery@hotmail.com. Open daily 10 A.M.–4 P.M. Visa and MasterCard accepted.

House of Water Crow opened in 1985 and contains an impressive range of arts and crafts, including acrylic and oil paintings, stone and wood carvings, micaceous pottery, traditional Native American weaponry, silver jewelry, beadwork, traditional clothing, leatherwork, animal fetishes, basketry, handmade sage-scented candles, and wood and clay flutes. **Carpio "Water Crow"** and family members create much of this work. Carpio developed his artistic and musical skills traveling with the **Native American Theater Ensemble** in the 1970s. Located next to the entrance booth. (505) 737-5901 or Water-Crow-2000@yahoo.com.

Songs of Indian Flute Shop features color photos and black-and-white prints on handmade paper by **Howard T. Rainer** and handmade wood flutes by his brother **John**. Howard's pictures have been published in three books, including *A Song for Mother Earth* and *Proud Moments*, as has his poetry in two volumes. Copies are available for sale in the shop. John's music is available on CD and cassette. The gallery also carries micaceous pottery by Taos and Acoma artisans, and a selection of jewelry. Located on the west side of the plaza. (505) 758-3103. Open daily 9 A.M.–5 P.M.

Hands on Silver carries jewelry by owner and artist **Wings**, including heishi necklaces, silver bracelets, pendants, and earrings. He also displays his handmade stone knives set in antler, beadwork by Navajo artisan **Volorie Willy**, micaceous pottery, and Sioux lances and canes. Located on the north side of the plaza. (505) 776-2555. Open daily 9 A.M.–4 P.M. Visa and MasterCard accepted.

Hlaukkwima is a good source of micaceous-clay storytellers made by the family of owner **Geraldine Lujan**. You can also order custom-made moccasins made by **Luke** and **Mildred Young** and pick up beaded necklaces. Located on the south side of the plaza. (505) 751-1235. Open 8 A.M.–5 P.M. in summer; otherwise hours vary.

Snowflake Flower Gift Shop carries a selection of necklaces, pendants, and stamped silverwork by Taos artisans. Located on the southwest corner of the plaza. (505) 751-1376.

Bobby Lujan is a Taos silversmith whose visage may be even better known than his jewelry, because he has been featured in major television and print commercials. His shop is located on the far southeast corner of the plaza. (505) 758-1840.

Jonathan Warm Day is a talented artist who works in serigraphs, cast paper, and acrylics. His images focus on life in the pueblo at the turn of the twentieth century, but his use of bold color and form are contemporary. Call (505) 751-1273 for an appointment.

Photographer **Bruce Gomez** produces award-winning color imagery of Taos Pueblo and environs. Prints are available framed or unframed, and can also be turned into large photomurals printed on ceramic tiles. To arrange an appointment, e-mail emanuelli@newmex.com.

Many Hands Tiwa Gift Shop, located in the **Taos Mountain Casino**, carries a small selection of Taos Pueblo-produced jewelry, pottery, paintings, beadwork, CDs and tapes, including some by the Taos-based **Indian House** label.

maker and musician John Rainer; and stone knife maker Wings. Several photographers also reside in Taos, including Bruce Gomez and Howard T. Rainer.

Diane Reyna, whose family operates one of the pueblo's finest galleries, began her arts career as a videographer, winning an Emmy for her work on the PBS program, "Surviving Columbus." She now creates original bronze sculpture, monotypes, and works in pastels.

Musician and major label recording artist Robert Mirabal (www.mirabal.com) combines traditional Native rhythms with up-tempo rock, folk, and jazz influences. He has toured in Europe and has been the subject of a PBS television special. Recent releases include *Taos Tales* (1999) and *Music From a Painted Cave* (2001).

Taos, like most pueblos, is home to an interesting adobe Catholic church, San Geronimo. Built in 1850, its altar contains a central image of the Virgin Mary, whom the Taos faithful also equate to Mother Earth. Parishioners change the clothing on the statues of the flanking saints according to the seasons.

Among the many ceremonial and secular events the residents host each year are the San Geronimo Feast Days, which attract visitors and extended family members from far and wide. The event begins on the evening of Sept. 29 with Catholic vespers and a sundown dance. The next day starts with a foot race at 8 A.M. Racers run east and west to symbolically empower the sun and moon. Intertribal dancers take over the plaza, while a trade fair operates on the perimeter. A highlight of the day is the arrival of the black-and-white-striped koshares, who serve as ceremonial clowns for the Pueblo culture and make fun of themselves, general human foibles, and audience members. Koshares attempt to climb a greased 75-foot pole erected on the plaza to reach treats placed on top. This feat, though it draws laughs from the crowd below, requires courage, athleticism, and stamina.

Unique among the pueblos, Taos also hosts all-Indian pow wows that feature fancy dancers, whose elaborate regalia originated among the Plains Indians. Such events commemorate Taos Pueblo's historic links to Plain Indian cultures.

TAOS

Must-see: Multistoried village, shops, artist studios, Wahleah's Gallery, Tony Reyna Indian Shop, Tiwa Kitchen, horseback ride, a ceremony

January 1 (morning and afternoon): turtle dances

January 6 (afternoon): deer or buffalo dance

May 3: Santa Cruz Feast Day, with foot race (8 A.M.) and corn dance (afternoon)

June 13: San Antonio Feast Day, with corn dances (afternoon)

June 24: San Juan Feast Day, with corn dances (afternoon)

July (second weekend): Taos Pueblo Pow Wow (photography allowed)

July 25-26: Santiago and Santa Ana Feast Days, with corn dances (afternoon)

September 29-30: San Geronimo Feast Days (see above)

December 24 (4-7 P.M.): Catholic vespers, bonfire procession of the Virgin Mary, and dances

December 25: deer or matachine dance

Taos Pueblo Tourism, P.O. Box 1846, Taos, NM 87571 (505) 758-1028 www.taospueblo.com

The site will include an on-line store of pueblo arts and crafts, schedule of feast and dance dates, and other helpful information.

TESUQUE

(tay-SOO-kay)

Te Tsugeh: "Narrow Place of Cottonwood Trees"

ALTHOUGH TESUQUE IS LOCATED very near Santa Fe, many visitors to northern New Mexico overlook this small pueblo in favor of its better-known Tewa-speaking pueblo neighbors of San Ildefonso or Santa Clara. But Tesuque is definitely worth a stop.

Set along the banks of Tesuque River, the two- and three-story adobe room blocks of Tesuque surround a small plaza and Catholic church. The traditional character of the pueblo is so well maintained that Tesuque is listed on the National Register of Historic Places. To the east rises the

beautiful Santa Fe range of the Sangre de Cristo Mountains. The reservation encompasses streamside fields and meadows, reddish tan foothills dotted with piñon and juniper, ponderosa pine forests, and, at the highest elevations, stands of Douglas fir, spruce, and quaking aspen. Only a five-minute drive from the jet-setting scene of Santa Fe, here the ancient orders and values linger.

History

The Tesuque Valley, with its dependable water supply and rich farmland, has long been a favored locale for human habitation. Archeological sites in the valley date back to at least A.D. 850, and may have been settled by emigrants from Chaco Canyon. By A.D. 1200, as many as a dozen small pueblos and hundreds of individual homes dotted the valley.

When the Spanish arrived in 1541, they found the population had consolidated into six villages, including the ancestral Tesuque, located about three miles east of the present village. Francisco Vásquez de Coronado estimated the community's population at one hundred seventy.

Tesuque residents played an important role in the Pueblo Revolt of 1680. Two messengers from Tesuque were captured by the Spanish and forced to reveal plans of the impending revolt. This breach prompted the conspiring pueblos to act swiftly. The next morning, warriors attacked and killed a Catholic priest from Santa Fe as he arrived at Tesuque to perform mass. Tesuque warriors participated in the subsequent siege of Santa Fe.

Feast day drummers, Tesuque
STEPHEN TRIMBLE

The pueblo's proximity to the Spanish capital of Santa Fe put the Tesuque people in a precarious position when the Spanish began their re-conquest campaign in 1692. In 1694, residents abandoned the old village, established a new one at the present site, and ceased overt hostilities against the Spanish.

But diseases introduced by the Spanish, loss of water rights and choice farmland, and other factors continued to erode the pueblo over the next few centuries, and by 1910 only seventy-seven inhabitants remained in Tesuque.

Contemporary Life

Since then, Tesuque's population has grown to about four hundred, and the residents have strengthened their culture and social customs.

A land base of 17,000 acres includes some farmland along the valley floor, hills dotted with juniper and piñon, and high mountain terrain carpeted in thick forests of pine and aspen.

The tribal government owns a popular flea market close to Santa Fe and a casino. Income is being used to build a new health facility and community center, to operate the tribe's Head Start

VISITING TESUQUE

DIRECTIONS: Located just five minutes north of **Santa Fe**. From **Santa Fe**, head north on US 84/285 for 7 1/2 miles. At mile marker 173.5, turn south (left) onto the village access road (Tribal Road 806), proceed across **Tesuque Creek**, turn right shortly thereafter to reach the village plaza and church. The Governor's Office is located about one-quarter mile west of the village entrance road on the south side of US 84/285.

PHOTOGRAPHY: Not allowed.

SKETCHING/SOUND RECORDING: Not allowed.

VISITOR CENTER/MUSEUM: None.

TOURS: None.

CASINO: **Camel Rock Casino** offers blackjack, poker, craps, roulette, Caribbean stud, bingo, and slots. (505) 984-8414 or (800) GO-CAMEL.

DINING: **Pueblo Artist Café** in Camel Rock Casino is a notably good and economical buffet-style restaurant, the best among the eight northern pueblos. It is well lit, isolated from the gaming rooms, and the staff is friendly and helpful. Nearby **Santa Fe** has many dining options.

ACCOMMODATIONS: The tribe owns the **Camel Rock Suites** in **Santa Fe**. (505) 989-3600.

CAMPING: Camping is not allowed.

RECREATION: Tesuque has a **fishing pond** that is stocked with four varieties of trout: rainbow, brook, cutbow, and German brown. Permits are available at the lake and cost $10 a day for adults and $5 for kids. It is usually open spring through fall.

The tribe also owns some beautiful acreage called **Aspen Ranch** in the **Sangre de Cristo Mountains** that includes a small stream, meadows, and aspen groves that make a fine place for picnicking and fishing. The tract is scheduled to reopen in 2003 after timber thinning and restoration work is completed.

ARTISTS AND GALLERIES: **Tewa Tioux Gallery** includes a selection of **Bea Tioux's** drums, as well as her outstanding pottery and Pueblo-style weavings and embroidery, Hopi and Navajo jewelry, and other items. Located on the plaza's southwest corner. (505) 989-9564. Open daily 9 A.M.–7 P.M. in summer, otherwise by appointment. Major credit cards are accepted.

A surprisingly large number of artists operate out of their homes here. They include the following:

Ignacia Duran is an accomplished potter who works in a large variety of ceramic formats, including big and small bowls and vases, pitchers, rain gods, and miniature animals such as frogs and deer. She also makes a storyteller coyote character. She works in copper-colored micaceous clay, polished blackware and redware, a white-slip-covered style painted with black, and black and red designs. Her rain gods come in three primary styles: a mica version, a traditional slip-covered and painted style, and an acrylic-painted form. (505) 983-7078. Cash and checks only.

Helen Herrera produces small bowls, animal and rain-god figurines, and Christmas ornaments. Most works are painted with acrylics, in sky and earth tones of blue, brown, beige, gray, and black. She occasionally produces traditional polished pottery pieces covered with a red slip. Open year round but call ahead. (505) 983-6730. Cash and checks only.

Terry Tapia specializes in miniature vessels and animal figurines, all done traditionally using a white slip painted with black-and-red designs. She also produces mid-sized animal figurines, and full-sized wedding vases by order. Her unique driftwood sculptures are dotted with miniature animal figurines, as are her turtle storyteller figurines, which depict a mother turtle covered with turtle babies. Call ahead. (505) 983-7075.

Bob Moquino produces bowls, wedding vases and other vessels, as well as pottery figurines of bears, turtles, and other animals. They are polished, covered with a white slip, and then painted with acrylics. His address is Rt. 35, Box 25 GP, Santa Fe, NM 87501.

and day-school programs, and for restoration of homes surrounding the village plaza. Tesuque maintains an organic commercial farm enterprise, and some tribal members farm small family plots. Most tribal residents work off the reservation in Santa Fe and elsewhere.

Art, Crafts, and Culture

More than twenty artisans work in Tesuque. The pueblo is perhaps best known for the production of so-called Rain Gods, small figurines of often brightly painted clay originally popularized by tourist in the early twentieth century. Today these figures are sometimes decorated with more traditional clay slip paints.

Potters, including Helen Herrera and Ignacia Duran, who operate small shops in the village, are among the pueblo's most active artisans. Others make their living making jewelry, painting, weaving, and beadworking.

Tesuque is also home to drummaker Bea Duran Tioux. "The art of drummaking is a very large part of our culture, the very heartbeat of all of us," says Bea, who has been creating these instruments since 1988. She makes handmade drums of many styles and sizes, all carved from aspen logs that she personally selects from tribal lands. Bea stretches hides of steer, deer, goat, and elk over each end of the drum and sews them tautly to achieve a warm, rich tone, and then applies decorative designs.

ZIA

(Tsee-ah)

Tsia

Crow dancers, Zia
PHOTOGRAPHER AND DATE UNKNOWN

Zia is off the usual tourist's route, but is a rewarding destination for those who seek it out. Set on a rocky ledge just above the wide Jemez River valley, with much of the native stone incorporated into its buildings, the pueblo is often overlooked by people speeding past on the nearby state highway.

Once one of the largest of all the pueblos, Zia was devastated by a series of calamities, and almost blinked out entirely at one point. But its people dug in and remain a vibrant community here at the base of the Jemez and Nacimiento mountains.

One of Zia's traditional design symbols, a circle with lines radiating outward in the four cardinal directions, was adopted by the New Mexico legislature as the official state emblem, and appears on the state flag.

The pueblo has a small but diverse community of artists working in both traditional and contemporary media. Its Catholic mission church, Nuestra Señora de la Asunción (Our Lady of the Assumption), was dedicated circa 1612 and may be the oldest operating Catholic parish in the United States.

History

The Zia people trace their roots to the Four Corners region. Their ancestors are believed to have migrated into the area near their present pueblo in the thirteenth century.

In 1583, Antonio de Espejo led a small exploratory party up the Rio Grande Valley from Mexico. Venturing up the Jemez River, Espejo encountered seven major pueblos, the inhabitants of whom he called Punames. The largest of these communities, Kowasaiya, was among the largest in the Pueblo realm. An estimated four thousand men, women, and children lived together in as many as eighteen hundred rooms.

"There are in this city five plazas, and many smaller ones," Espejo's scribe recorded. "The homes are of three and four stories, and well arranged. The people are clean. The women wear a blanket over their shoulders tied with a sash at the waist—their hair cut in front, and the rest plaited so that it forms two braids, and above a blanket of turkey feathers."

In 1681 and 1687, following the Pueblo Revolt, Spanish forces returned to the area and attacked the pueblo, but were repulsed. In 1688, a larger force returned and again attacked. This time, the Spanish succeeded in their assault, burning the pueblo, killing scores and taking hundreds captive. When the Spanish returned for good in 1692 under Diego de Vargas, the people of Zia pledged loyalty to the crown and ceased all overt hostilities toward the colonizers.

However, raids by nomadic tribes, including Navajo and Ute, resulted in further losses of territory and lives. Various diseases introduced first by the Spanish and then by Anglo Americans in the 1800s also took their toll, and by the 1890s the tribe's population stood at just ninety-eight people.

Contemporary Life

Today, the Zia tribe numbers nearly eight hundred people, and members continue to speak their native tongue—Keres. The tribe has chosen not to develop gaming or a tourism-oriented economy, but is pursuing other interesting endeavors, including the development of a community plaza in the largely Hispanic town of Bernalillo.

The tribe also owns 75 acres in the center of the small town of San Ysidro, five miles west of the village, where it is developing commercial lease and rental properties. Long-term plans call for a tribal visitor center here, including displays of traditional homes, arts and crafts sales, and an RV park.

Tribal members graze cattle and farm fields flanking the Rio Jemez. Corn, chiles, and other vegetables are used for family consumption and for ceremonial purposes. A large gypsum mine also operates on the reservation.

Reservation land—in two separate tracts—covers about 122,000 acres, ranging in elevation from 5,200 feet to over 9,000 feet and thus encompassing a range of ecological zones. Bear, elk, deer, beaver, cougar, and even the rare, native Rio Grande cutthroat trout still thrive in the mountainous terrain. Below, on the desert-like flats and foothills, live coyotes, cottontails, jackrabbits, prairie dogs, and lizards.

If the landscape looks somewhat familiar, perhaps you've seen the films *Ghosts of Mars*, *All the Pretty Horses*, or the television show *Earth 2*. All were filmed wholly or in part on Zia lands.

VISITING ZIA

DIRECTIONS: Located 35 miles northwest of **Albuquerque**. From **Albuquerque**, head north on I-25 to **Bernalillo**, and Exit onto NM 44. Proceed west 17 miles and turn right onto the village access road.

VISITOR CENTER/MUSEUM: The tribe operates a small but informative **Cultural Center** with displays of pre-historic and historic Zia artifacts (including stone tools and cotton and yucca-fiber sandals), arts, and historic and contemporary photographs. The center is located next to the **Governor's Office**, just off the village access road. Open weekdays 8 A.M.–noon and 1 P.M.–5 P.M. Admission is free.

TOURS: None.

PHOTOGRAPHY: Not allowed.

SKETCHING/SOUND RECORDING: Not allowed.

DINING: The nearest restaurants are in **Bernalillo**.

ACCOMMODATIONS: None; the nearest hotels are in **Bernalillo** and **Albuquerque**.

CAMPING: Not allowed.

RECREATION: A 30-acre shallow lake provides **year round angling** for catfish in hot and warm months and trout in winter. The site presents dramatic views of the surrounding terrain, and the lake itself is flanked by cattails, tall sunflowers, and small cottonwood trees. The site offers picnic ramadas and restrooms. The lake is located 2.5 miles west of the village on the north side of the river, along a gravel road. Fishing permits are $6 per day for adults, $3 for kids under twelve. Rowboats are allowed, and cost $5 per day. Obtain permits at a pay station on the access road.

ARTISTS AND GALLERIES: The **Cultural Center** displays locally produced work and can provide artist contact information, including a village map showing studio/home locations. None of the homes are marked with commercial signs, but they are well marked with street numbers that correspond to the map available from the **Cultural Center**.

Art, Crafts, and Culture

Considering its size, Zia has a surprisingly large number of artists working in a wide range of media. In 1954, Zia painter Velino Herrera was awarded a prestigious Palmes Academiques by the French government for outstanding work. However, the pueblo's artisans are probably best known for their pottery, and the design element most associated with Zia is a big-eyed bird with a split tail, often done in an outline form of black filled in with an orange color over a light tan base.

Split-tailed bird pot by Candelaria Gachupin, Zia
STEPHEN TRIMBLE

Perhaps the most celebrated potters at Zia are the Medina family. Sofia Medina creates very large ollas. Her daughter-in-law, Elizabeth Medina, does exquisite traditional Zia work, while her husband Marcellus paints delicate, detailed designs in acrylics on vessels made by Elizabeth. He also does fine paintings on canvas and paper. Other active pottery families include the Shijes, Piños, and Toribios.

Artisans are also active in textile and basket weaving, painting, stone carving and flint knapping. Juanico Galvan produces unique woven hair ties, while Anacita Archuleta's apparel includes lovely embroidered mantas for girls. Zia is one of the few pueblos with active basket weavers, whose ranks include former governor Amadeo Shije. Ralph Aragon specializes in painted gourds, while Bob Gachupin, Clifford Lucero, and Antonio Medina create stone carvings. Tribal members, including tribal administrator Peter Piño, also make traditional arrowheads, and bow and arrows.

The pueblo's beautiful church, Nuestra Señora de la Asunción, was damaged but not destroyed in the Pueblo Revolt of 1680, making it one of the nation's most historic. It has a striking facade—its door flanked by murals of a white and a yellow horse and swallows in flight. These little birds are still seen whizzing past the church on a typical day. The church's packed earth floor, absence of pews, and painted wood altar leave a simple but lasting impression.

ZUNI

(Zoo-nee)

She-we-na: "The Middle Place"

ZUNI IS THE PUEBLO DIFFERENT. Although culturally, socially, and religiously related to the eighteen other pueblos in New Mexico, Zuni stands apart. Located west of the Continental Divide—south of Gallup, New Mexico, and near the Arizona border—Zuni is far removed from the pueblos of the Rio Grande Valley. The Zuni people also speak a distinctive language and their pueblo also is the largest, both in land area (418,000 acres) and in population (10,500 residents).

This is a land of plateaus and mesas that tower as high as several thousand feet above wide valleys and plains. Bounded on the north by the Zuni Mountains, a range that tops out at more than 8,000 feet and boasts dense forests of ponderosa pine and Douglas fir, the land slopes generally from north to south. Runoff from the Zuni Mountains watershed feeds numerous small streams. These once flowed directly into the Zuni River, which ran through Zuni village and provided ample water to irrigate the community's farms downstream. Today, except when fed by late summer cloudbursts, the Zuni River is dry. In summer, daytime temperatures at Zuni seldom exceed 100 degrees, but winters can be surprisingly cold, and snow often drapes the ancient adobe parapets.

Throughout their history, the Zuni people have wielded considerable power and influence in the region, and today their distinctive culture and artistic sensibilities are recognized and appreciated by visitors from every corner of the globe. Indeed, Zuni artisans produce more fine traditional Pueblo art and craft items than their counterparts at any other pueblo. Perhaps 75 percent of the Zuni populace makes a living from some form of art. Casual tourists and serious collectors alike particularly cherish Zuni silver jewelry and carved stone animal fetishes.

History

Zuni may be the oldest pueblo in New Mexico. Pithouses, some dating to A.D. 700, and many other remnants of early Zuni settlements dot the region and attest to the long-term presence of the Zuni people in this locale. (Deserted masonry dwellings include Atsinna at nearby El Morro National Monument.) The Zuni people grew corn, beans, melons, squashes, and many other vegetables on large, irrigated farms. They supplemented this diet with game from the mountains and plains.

The present village, Halona Idi:wanna (Middle Place), has been occupied continuously since the 1690s. Ten miles to the southwest of Halona Idi:wanna lie the remains of Hawikku. This was the first pueblo that Fray Marcos de Niza

Dowa Yallane, Zuni
STEPHEN TRIMBLE

right: Costume contestant from Zuni at Indian Market, Santa Fe
MARK NOHL

Waffle gardens, Zuni, 1911
JESSE L. NUSSBAUM

and his subordinate, Esteban, encountered in 1539, when they became the first Spaniards to venture north from Mexico into what is now the American Southwest. Esteban's dark complexion intrigued his reluctant hosts, but his ill manners ultimately led to his demise at the hands of the Zuni people. His death proved to be no deterrent to the Spanish.

Fray Marcos returned to Mexico with fantastic tales of riches to the north, and the following year Zuni was the first pueblo to succumb to armed conquest led by Francisco Vásquez de Coronado during his ill-fated entrada to find the friar's fabled Seven Cities of Cibola. But it wasn't until 1598 that Spanish soldiers, settlers, and missionaries arrived to establish a permanent presence in New Mexico.

Zuni warriors participated in the 1680 Pueblo Revolt and subsequently took refuge on Dowa Yallane, the high mesa that lies southeast of Halona Idi:wanna. In 1692, the Spanish returned in force to re-establish control in New Mexico.

Zuni authorities made peace with the Spanish and, except for the presence of a Catholic mission, the pueblo maintained its autonomy.

Contemporary Life

The Zuni people acquired sheep, horses, and cattle from the Spanish, and grazing and animal husbandry became major economic mainstays of the pueblo by the late eighteenth century. Today, Zuni grazing lands provide meager forage and can no longer support many head of livestock. Herding provides only a minor source of income, as does timber harvesting. Arable land likewise is limited, so farming too has fallen off dramatically. Instead, the arts have become the mainstay of the Zuni economy.

Like other pueblos, Zuni has both a traditional elder council that oversees spiritual observances and settles minor legal issues and disputes among residents of the pueblo, and an elected secular government that deals with the outside world. Elections for governor are held every four years.

VISITING ZUNI

DIRECTIONS: The village of Zuni is located 30 miles south of **Gallup** on NM 53. It is accessible from all four directions, but most visitors use the northern approach from **Gallup** via NM 62; or from the east via NM 53. This is the lovely **Grants-through-Ramah** route, which passes **El Morro National Monument** and other major landmarks.

VISITOR CENTER/MUSEUM: Stop at the excellent **visitor center**, which includes the **A:shiwi A:wan Museum and Heritage Center**. The center has informative displays on Zuni's rich history, including historic black-and-white photographs, a captivating mural of the Zuni creation story painted by Zuni artists, and exhibitions of cultural artifacts. One can also obtain a map of the Zuni village, photo permits, and other information helpful for a Zuni visit. Behind the center is the tribal museum, which displays changing exhibitions by and for the Zuni people, such as an exhibition about Zuni veterans and a display of contemporary art inspired by cultural motifs associated with the Zuni ancestral home **Hawikku**. A small patio contains a garden of native plants, and hornos and fire pits where you may happen upon a feast being prepared.

The **visitor center** is located on the east side of the village at 1222 NM 53. It is open fall through spring Mon.–Fri., and summer Mon.–Sat., 9 A.M.–5:30 P.M. Admission is free, although a $5 museum donation is suggested.

TOURS: The **visitor center** conducts guided tours to see historical architecture, flora and fauna, and Zuni artists at work. Reservations should be made in advance.

PHOTOGRAPHY: Except at the visitor center, photography is only allowed with a permit. Certain areas and events are restricted. Camera permits are available at the visitor center and are $10 for video, $5 for stills. Ask about photo-restricted areas within the village.

SKETCHING/SOUND RECORDING: Allowed only at events held at the **visitor center**.

DINING: Chu-Chu's Pizzeria offers pizza, calzones, lasagna, fried chicken, hamburgers, and subs. Located on NM 53 at the east edge of town. (505) 782-2100. Open daily for lunch and dinner.

Route 53 Café serves New Mexican dishes—such as a renowned green and red chile—and American fare; group meals can be arranged with advance notice. Located at the town's only four-way stop, 1169 NM 53, (505) 782-4404. Open late fall–spring Mon.–Thurs. 9 A.M.–9 P.M., Fri.–Sat. 9 A.M.–10 P.M., closed Sun.; summer Mon.–Thurs. 8 A.M.–10 P.M., Fri.–Sat. 8 A.M.–11 P.M., Sun. 8 A.M.–5 P.M. All major credit cards accepted.

Major Market has a small dining area and serves New Mexican dishes, grilled sandwiches, chicken dinners, and take-out deli items. Located at 1229 NM 53. (505) 782-5571. The deli is open daily 11 A.M.–4 P.M.

Halona Plaza Market on Pia Mesa Road also has a small dining area and serves take-out sandwiches, fried chicken, and potato salad. Other options for light snacks and fast food include B.L. Bakery, and Lemon Tree Snack Bar.

ACCOMMODATIONS: The only option in the village is **The Inn at Halona**, but this five-bedroom, three-level, pueblo-style bed-and-breakfast is a rare treat. Rooms are decorated with Zuni and Southwestern art, and very comfortable beds. There are four baths, a central living room with cast-iron gas fireplace, covered and open outdoor patio space, room phones, fax and satellite TV, and room service. In an adjoining building are another three rooms with a larger meeting space, patio, and upstairs deck. Base rates are $79 per night for a single room, but vary according to season, length of stay, and number of rooms needed. Be sure to call or e-mail ahead for reservations: (505) 782-4547, (800) 752-3278, or www.halona.com.

Forty-five miles east of Zuni village on NM 53 is another bed-and-breakfast called **Cimarron Rose**. (800) 856-5776 or cimarronrose.com.

Gallup has numerous places to stay.

CAMPING: One corner of the Zuni reservation lies in the beautiful **Zuni Mountains**. The **Nutria Lakes** dot a major valley that wends out of the forested slopes. The tribal campground at one of the larger lakes has fire pits and outhouses and is open to the public. Turn north off NM 53 a few miles east of NM 602 onto BIA Road 5 and proceed 7 miles. A $5 nightly permit, available in the village or by mail, is

required. For permits or details, call (505) 782-5851.

RECREATION: Fishing with a permit is allowed at the **Nutria**, **Ojo Caliente** (southwest of Zuni village on BIA Road 2), **Estace**, and **Pescado** lakes. **Hunting** permits for small and big game, including deer and elk, also are available. Contact the Zuni Dept. of Fish and Wildlife, (505) 782-5851.

ARTISTS AND GALLERIES: Along Zuni's main street, NM 53, you'll find a number of arts and crafts shops, some of which are owned and operated by Zuni merchants, others by non-tribal members.

Attached to the visitor center is the **Zuni Arts and Crafts Enterprise**, which is owned and operated by the pueblo. Here you will find a wide array of high-quality goods, including exquisite fetishes, rings, earrings, necklaces, bracelets, bolos, pendants, studs, crosses, and beaded jewelry. The shop also features rarely produced Zuni katsina dolls; traditional and "contemporary" (slip-poured and hand finished) pottery vessels and figurines; woven sashes and other apparel; and paintings and other wall art. There is also an assortment of Native American music, including works by Zuni flautist **Fernando Cellicion** and the **Zuni Midnighters**, and books on Zuni arts and history. (505) 782-5531. Major credit cards are accepted.

Zuni Craftsman Cooperative Association is a nonprofit, artist-directed shop opened in 1967. Though tucked into humble quarters, it presents a top-notch selection of all forms of Zuni arts and crafts produced by its 525 members. Jewelry and fetishes predominate, but the shop also displays a fine selection of pottery and beadwork. Jewelry includes work by **Smokey**, who makes unusual use of chunk coral, and members of the **Quandelacy** family, who contribute fetish necklaces and standing fetishes. Visa, MasterCard and American Express credit cards are accepted. The shop is located at 1177 NM 53. (505) 782-4425 or (888) 926-1842.

Other recommended commercial shops, all of which accept major credit cards, include the following: **Turquoise Village** features a large selection of pottery, mostly by Hopi, Acoma, and Zuni artisans, rings and

(continues on next page)

VISITING ZUNI

(continued from page 93)

other jewelry, stone fetishes and corn maidens by the **Quandelacy** family, and some Hopi katsinas. Located at 1184 NM 53. (800) 748-2405. Closed Sundays.

Pueblo Trading Post has been in existence more than twenty years with nice displays of historic pictures mixed with antiques and the works for sale, which include mostly fine Zuni creations in a diverse array of jewelry forms and some pottery, as well as a selection of antique Apache baskets. Located at 1192 NM 53. (505) 782-2296. Open daily.

Running Bear Trading Post has a selection of Zuni and Navajo work including a large collection of earrings, bracelets, and necklaces, as well as fetishes, katsina dolls, and some pottery—such as the vessels by **Marcus Homer** with raised frog figures. Located at 1239 NM 53, on the east side of the village. (505) 782-5505.

Just north of Zuni is **Joe Milo's Trading Company**, which carries a large selection of Zuni, Hopi, and Navajo jewelry and jeweler supplies. Located a 1628 S. Hwy 602 in Vandenberg. (505) 778-5531.

A number of artists also show their work in their homes, and many feature art objects created by other Zuni artisans.

D.Y. Jewelry features the prize-winning jewelry of **Loren Panteah** and **Yo Laate**, especially items with four-point star designs and channel inlay sun faces composed of turquoise, red coral, lapis, sugilite, green gaspeite, orange spiny oyster shell, white mother of pearl, and opal. Located on the far eastern edge of the village at 1449A NM 53. (505) 782-2454.

Silverbear Studio and Gallery specializes in hollow silver bears fashioned into earrings, pendants, and necklaces by **Carlton Jamon**. He also makes pendants and earrings with petroglyph designs in silver, gold and various stones. The gallery also features hand-cast paper with natural dyes by **Julie Jamon** and paintings, prints, pottery, jewelry, and fetishes by other Zuni artists. Located at 32 Pia Mesa Rd. (505) 782-2869 or silverbearstudio.com. Closed Mondays.

Creative Hands carries award-winning artist **Noreen Simplicio's** traditionally made bowls, vases, miniatures and seed bowls decorated with traditional Zuni designs and contemporary elements, including fine lines, birds, crawling lizard figurines, and animal symbols. The gallery also features jewelry created by her mother **Carmelita**. Located at 20A Chavez Rd. (505) 782-2543 or creativehands-99@yahoo.com.

Silver Rain Studio features silverwork by **Ferdinand** and **Sylvia Hooee**. Located at 1449B NM 53.

Andres Quandelacy, a member of a talented Zuni fetish carving family, creates charming and novel figurines, such as a green turquoise bear with a pink coral fish in its mouth. P.O. Box 266, Zuni, NM 87327.

Ricky Laahty is a talented young fetish carver who specializes in frogs. P.O. Box 274, Zuni, NM (505) 782-4791.

Yet another pair of notable fetish carvers is **Gibbs** and **Bobbie Othole**, who focus on miniatures in lapis, veracite, red coral, amber, and other unusual materials. (505) 782-5892.

Art, Crafts, and Culture

Zuni has a remarkable artistic tradition. Artisans were creating simple jewelry more than a thousand years ago, and by the early 1800s Zuni craftsmen were making sophisticated jewelry from copper and brass. In the early 1870s, Navajo master silversmith Atsidi Chon shared his expertise with Lanyade, a Zuni artist who in turn introduced the new process to Zuni.

Zuni jewelers are among the finest in the world, and are particularly renowned for setting stone and shell in sterling silver. They employ a wide variety of techniques, including mosaic overlay and inlay, channel inlay, cluster and row work, petit point and needlepoint, and nugget style. Coral, turquoise, and mother-of-pearl are among the favorite materials used, but artisans also work with a wide range of other semiprecious and precious stones, shells, animal horn, and wood. They produce a great range of jewelry forms, including bracelets, rings, earrings, necklaces, pendants, and

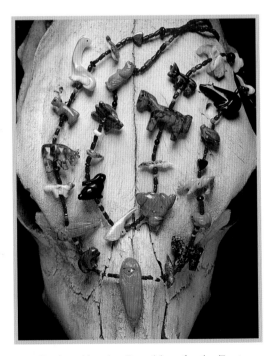

Fetish necklace by Quandelacy family, Zuni

MARK NOHL

bolos. Some artists work in strictly traditional forms and materials, while others create cutting-edge contemporary designs using unconventional materials and gold settings. Carolyn Bobelu (known for her intricate mosaic inlay of turquoise, coral, jet, and shell) and Edith Tsabetsaye (famous for her incredible needlepoint work) are among the many contemporary jewelry masters whose work is highly prized.

Carved animal fetishes are Zuni's second most popular art form. Traditional fetishes depicted animals native to the region, but today carvers may portray almost any creature. Once blessed, the fetish is believed to carry the spirit and supernatural qualities of the animal it represents. Fetishes are most often carved from stone, but they also may be created from shell, wood, and antler.

While not as well known for pottery as the artisans of Santa Clara or San Ildefonso, many Zuni potters produce outstanding work. Traditional design elements found on bowls and pots include tadpoles (representing spring), dragonflies and butterflies (symbolizing summer), and frogs (connoting winter). Many artists work in painting and drawing media as well.

Zuni also maintains another traditional Pueblo craft—weaving—which virtually has disappeared from the other pueblos, and its residents are the only ones outside of the Hopi who produce katsina dolls.

The Zuni people also practice an active ceremonial and religious life. Unlike the other pueblos, Zuni does not observe a Feast Day, and traditional ceremonies are generally closed to the public.

At Zuni, ancient and adopted faith traditions are celebrated at Nuestra Señora de Guadalupe, a mission church originally built in 1629 and extensively restored in the 1960s by the National Park Service and Catholic diocese. The interior of this classic New Mexico adobe mission, which some admirers call the "Sistine Chapel of the Americas," is truly remarkable. Elaborate and beautiful murals—depicting nearby landmarks, the four seasons, and life-size Zuni katsinam—adorn the walls. Zuni artist Alex Seowtewa began painting these murals in 1970, and he and his sons continue to labor over them today.

ZUNI

Must-see: The A:shiwi A:wan Museum and Heritage Center, Guadalupe Mission, arts and craft shops and studios, Nutria Lakes

Unlike other pueblos, Zuni holds no annual Feast Day. Other major events open to the public are listed below. Call for exact dates.

April: Earth Day Festival

August (second weekend): Zuni Arts Expo

August (third weekend): Zuni Fair

October: Harvest Festival

late November to mid-December (annually one night): Shalako, impressive, public sacred ceremony involving many elaborately dressed figures

Visitor Center,
P.O. Box 1009, Zuni, NM 87327
or
Pueblo of Zuni,
P.O. Box 339, Zuni, NM 87327
Visitor Center, (505) 782-4403
Governor's Office, (505) 782-4481
aamhc@zuni.k12.nm.us

The church is usually open weekdays 9 A.M.–4 P.M. and is located near the center of the old village. To get there, turn south onto Pia Mesa Road at the four-way stop on NM 53. Turn east (left) onto Sunset (parallel to the river) and then north (left) on Mission Street.

overleaf: Detail of Katsinam mural by Alex Seowtewa, Nuestra Señora de Guadalupe Catholic church, Zuni

MARK NOHL

Calendar of Pueblo Events

THROUGHOUT THE YEAR, each pueblo marks the passing of seasons and the annual cycle of life with a series of ceremonial dances. Some—including those noted below—are open to the public.

Winter dances generally honor animals whose meat and fur help sustain the people through the bitterly cold winter months, while late spring, summer, and fall dances honor the plant kingdom, and in particular that most important food staple: corn.

All of the pueblos except Zuni celebrate "feast days" that honor the pueblos' patron Catholic saints. Several pueblos encompass multiple villages, each with its own church and feast day. Some pueblos also celebrate saint days that are more closely associated with other pueblos.

Feast days tend to be the most popular public events in a pueblo's annual cycle for Indian and non-Indian visitors alike. Most feast days actually begin the evening before with a mass or benediction, perhaps a procession, followed by a morning mass. Pueblo artists and craftsmen take advantage of these festive occasions to display and sell their goods. Food and beverages can also be purchased at most feast day events.

Most pueblo churches celebrate Christmas mass, and many of these observances are open to nonresidents. Many pueblos also stage elaborate processions at Christmas and Easter. Some northern pueblos conduct matachines dances, in which veiled participants combine elements of the morality plays of medieval Spain with traditional pueblo stories.

Pueblos also hold dances that are not publicized, but are open to the public. Be aware that dances and ceremonies announced as open to the public are subject to change or closure without notice.

Note: TBA means "to be announced."

JANUARY
1: Transfer of the Canes. On this day at many pueblos, including most of the eight northern pueblos, outgoing governors pass these historic symbols of secular authority to their successors. Residents perform various dances, including the turtle dance at Taos and the corn dance at Cochiti.
6: King's Day Celebration. The election of new officers is marked with dances at most pueblos, including buffalo, deer and antelope at Picuris and Nambe, corn at San Felipe, and buffalo or deer at San Juan, Sandia, Pojoaque, and Taos. Dances performed elsewhere include eagle and elk.
23: San Ildefonso Feast Day. Presentation of a buffalo and Comanche dance precedes the evening firelight dances. No food or arts booths.
25: San Paulo Feast Day celebrated at Picuris with various dances.
Late January (TBA): San Juan cloud or basket dance.

FEBRUARY
2: Candelaria Day celebrated at Picuris with various dances.
Early February (TBA): Governor's Feast Day celebrated at Acoma.
Late February (TBA): San Juan deer dances.
February/March: Taos Pueblo is usually closed to all visitors. Inquire.

MARCH
19: San José Feast Day celebrated at Old Laguna.
Easter Sunday: Various dances, including basket and corn, conducted at many pueblos. Dances occur at Zia on Easter Sunday and the following three days. Mass celebrated in Acomita and McCarty on the Acoma Reservation.

APRIL
(TBA): Earth Day Festival celebrated at Zuni.

MAY
First Sunday: Santa María Feast Day celebrated at McCarty, Acoma Reservation.
1: San Felipe Feast Day: Various pueblos perform the corn dance.
3: Santa Cruz Feast Day celebrated with the corn dance at Cochiti, footraces and corn dance at Taos, and various dances at Zia.
Memorial Day weekend: Jemez Red Rocks Arts and Crafts Show, on NM 4 south of the Walatowa Visitor Center, Jemez Reservation.

JUNE
First Saturday of June: Tesuque blessing of the fields and corn dance; and Native American Appreciation Day, Ellis Tanner Trading Company, Gallup, (505) 863-4434.
13: San Antonio Feast Day celebrated at Sandia with a corn dance. Also corn dances at Taos, Picuris, Santa Clara, and San Juan, and a Comanche dance at San Ildefonso.
Third weekend of June: New Governor Honoring Day at Isleta.
24: San Juan Bautista Feast Day at San Juan with Comanche dances; corn and/or buffalo and Comanche dances at Taos, and corn dance at Santa Ana.
29: San Pedro Feast Day celebrated with corn dance at Santa Ana and Acoma.
Last weekend of June: High Country Arts & Crafts Festival at Picuris.

JULY
4: Nambe Falls Celebration, Nambe.
Second weekend of July: Taos Pueblo Pow Wow.
14: San Buenaventura Feast Day celebrated at Cochiti with corn dance.
Mid July: Eight Northern Pueblos Arts and Crafts Festival, usually held at San Juan Pueblo. Some fifteen hundred artists and craftsmen gather to display a great range of unique, handcrafted, traditional and contemporary Native American art. Founded in 1971, this is the largest Native-run, juried arts festival in the world. The show also includes Indian dances accompanied by singers and drummers, and native foods. Still photography ($10 pass) is allowed. Entry fee is $5 for adults or $8 for a two-day pass. The festival kicks off with

a benefit reception and live and silent auction of Indian art and services in Santa Fe. (800) 793-4955 or www.artnewmexico.com/eightnorthern),

25: Feast Day of Santiago celebrated with corn dances at Santa Ana, Acoma, San Ildefonso, and Taos.

26: Santa Ana Feast Day celebrated at Santa Ana with corn dances, as well as at Taos, and at Laguna Pueblo.

AUGUST

4: Santo Domingo Feast Day celebrated at Santo Domingo with a corn dance.

10: San Lorenzo Feast Day celebrated at Picuris and Acomita on the Acoma Reservation.

12: Santa Clara Feast Day celebrated at Santa Clara.

Second weekend of August: Gallup Intertribal Indian Ceremonial. This is the granddaddy of all Southwest Indian festivals. Founded in 1921, the Gallup Intertribal Indian Ceremonial set the standard for pan-Indian arts and cultural festivals that today occur throughout the nation, and none can yet match the Gallup ceremonial's range of events. These include the Southwest's largest all-Indian rodeo, a major fine arts show, pow wow and traditional dancing, an arts and crafts market, traditional Native foods, and Indian parades.

The juried art show includes work in nine classes: pottery, Navajo weavings, baskets, katsina dolls and carved figures, jewelry and flatware, tribal arts (including pipes, rattles, totem poles, beaded dresses), paintings, sculpture, and juvenile entries. It is considered the best venue in the world for viewing Navajo textiles. In addition, the artists also display and sell arts and crafts in the large indoor and outdoor markets.

No celebration would be complete without a parade, and the ceremonial hosts a major all-Indian, non-mechanized parade with horse-drawn floats and wagons, dancers, and marchers. Parades are held in downtown Gallup.

All other ceremonial events take place at Red Rocks State Park just east of Gallup. General admission costs $3 for adults and $1 for children. Reserved-seat admission to the dance events (which also covers general admission), costs $20 for adults and $10 for children. Non-reserved seats are half price. Admission to the rodeo costs $8 for adults and $4 for children. (800) 233-4528 or www.gallupceremonial.com

Second weekend of August: Zuni Arts and Crafts Expo.

15: Feast Day of Nuestra Señora de la Asunción celebrated at Zia with

morning mass, a procession, and corn dances; and at Mesita, Laguna, with various dances.

Third weekend of August: Santa Fe Indian Market. The premiere Indian arts and culture festival in the nation finds more than twelve hundred Indian artisans and craftspeople mingling with art collectors from around the world. Serious and casual collectors alike come to admire and buy a wide range of pottery, jewelry, carved wood and stone sculpture, and visual arts ranging from painting and prints to photography. Also in demand are textile arts (weaving and clothing), drums, and beadwork. The smell of popular Navajo frybread wafts through the air while musicians and dancers fill the streets with sound and motion. Indian Market always begins with a Friday evening preview of award-winning works for members of the host organization (the Southwestern Association for Indian Arts) in Santa Fe's Sweeney Center, and a silent auction of select Market artists.

The artists booths are open 7 A.M. to 5 P.M. Saturdays, and from 8 A.M. to 5 P.M. Sundays. Food booths are located in the Sweeney Center parking lot, while children's activities and art demonstrations are held in shady Cathedral Park. Saturday evening features the main social event of the festival, a cocktail party with appetizers and silent and live auctions. You'll also find almost every gallery in town hosting special exhibitions (mostly by Indian artists) and receptions throughout the weekend. Nightclubs often book Native bands, and parties run late. Running concurrently is the Native Roots and Rhythms Festival, featuring major Indian musical and dance groups, which is held at the Paolo Soleri outdoor amphitheater. (505) 983-5220 or www.swaia.org.

Third weekend of August: Zuni Tribal Fair with parade, midway, Indian pro rodeo, pow wow, arts and crafts, live music and performing entertainment, barbecue, country-western dances, races, and athletic tournaments. (505) 782-2900.

28: San Agustín Feast Day celebrated at Isleta.

Late August/Early September: San Ildefonso corn dance.

Labor Day weekend: Santo Domingo Arts and Crafts Show.

SEPTEMBER

2: San Estevan Feast Day celebrated in Acoma's "Sky City."

4: Morning procession from church and afternoon dances at Isleta.

8: Navidad de María Feast Day celebrated at San Ildefonso with corn dances.

19: San José Feast Day celebrated at Old Laguna with buffalo, corn, and eagle dances.

25: Feast Day at Paguate, Laguna, celebrated with buffalo, corn, eagle, harvest, and social dances.

29: Vespers and sundown dances at Taos.

30: San Geronimo Feast Day celebrated at Taos.

Last week of September: San Juan harvest dances.

OCTOBER

TBA: Zuni Harvest Festival.

4: San Francisco de Asís Feast Day celebrated at Nambe.

Second weekend of October: Bien Mur Marketfest, Sandia.

17: San Margarita María Feast Day celebrated at Paguate, Laguna.

NOVEMBER

12: San Diego Feast Day celebrated at Tesuque.

Mid-November to mid-December: Zuni Shalako ceremony.

DECEMBER

First weekend of December: Winter Arts and Crafts Show at Jemez Civic Center.

12: Nuestra Señora de Guadalupe Feast Day at Pojoaque celebrated with various dances, and arts and craft sales.

24: Christmas Eve. Various dances and events, including sundown pine torchlight processions at Picuris, Taos, San Juan, and Tesuque; and dances after mass, including a buffalo dance around a bonfire at Nambe, matachines dances at Taos and Picuris, and Isleta, harvest and arrow dances at Laguna, and various other dances at Sandia. Acoma residents celebrate Christmas with a luminaria display and mass at San Estevan.

25: Christmas Day. Each pueblo celebrates Christmas with its own particular dance tradition, including matachines at San Juan and Picuris, and buffalo at Zia. Dances vary at Santa Clara, Taos, San Ildefonso, Tesuque, Cochiti, Sandia, Santa Ana, San Felipe, Isleta, Acoma.

26: San Juan Turtle Dance, at Acoma, Zia, and Isleta.

27: Various dances at Acoma, Isleta, Laguna, and Zia.

28: Holy Innocents Day, with children's dances at various pueblos, including Santa Clara and Picuris. Other dances are performed at Acoma, Isleta, Laguna, and Zia.

Museums and Cultural Centers

A number of museums and cultural centers, located near the nineteen Pueblo reservations in New Mexico's major cities, provide excellent insights into Pueblo culture, arts, and history.

INDIAN PUEBLO CULTURAL CENTER

This is a great place to introduce yourself to New Mexico's Pueblo Indians. The center, opened in 1976, is owned and run by the Pueblo peoples, and this alone makes it unique. Here you can tour permanent exhibits on the arts and history of each of the pueblos, see changing contemporary art shows, watch live dances and arts and crafts demonstrations on weekends and most holidays, and even take in a meal—all in the Indian way. The center also houses a children's museum, an excellent gift shop, and a bookstore that carries children's books, Indian magazines, and newspapers. The gift shop carries a wide range of goods, particularly Pueblo pottery and jewelry, as well Navajo rugs and silver jewelry, Hopi katsinas, baskets by the Tohono O'odham of Arizona, and some Plains Indian goods.

Details: Located in Albuquerque at 2401 12th St. NW. Exit 157B north from I-40 to the intersection of 12th Street NW and Indian School Road. Open daily (except Christmas) 9 A.M.–5:30 P.M. Admission is $4 for adults, $3 seniors, and $1 for students. Children under six free. (505) 843-7270, (800) 766-4405, or www.indianpueblo.org

INSTITUTE OF AMERICAN INDIAN ARTS MUSEUM

This museum, known locally as the IAIA Museum, showcases work from the nation's premier Indian arts educational facility. It houses a superb collection of more than eight thousand contemporary Indian art works by Allan Houser, T.C. Cannon, Charles Loloma, Doug Hyde, Fritz Scholder, Earl Biss, Linda Lomahaftewa, Denise Wallace, and other alumni and faculty members. Don't overlook the sculpture garden. The museum displays traveling and revolving exhibitions and houses an outstanding gift shop with fine arts, jewelry, music selections, and books.

Details: Located in Santa Fe, across the street from St. Francis Cathedral at 108 Cathedral Pl.

Open Mon.–Sat. 10 A.M.–5 P.M., Sun 12 A.M.–5 P.M. Admission is $4 for adults and $2 for students and seniors. Children under sixteen free. (505) 983-8900 or www.iaiancad.org

MAXWELL MUSEUM OF ANTHROPOLOGY

This small but well-managed facility offers surprisingly rich collections of Southwest Native American arts and artifacts, as well as works of other world cultures. The museum has both permanent and changing exhibitions.

Details: Located on the campus of the University of New Mexico in Albuquerque. Open Tues.–Fri. 9 A.M.–4 P.M.; Sat. 10 A.M.–4 P.M. Closed Sun.–Mon. and major holidays. Free. (505) 277-4405 or www.maxwell@unm.edu/~maxwell

MILLICENT ROGERS MUSEUM

This excellent, relatively small museum displays works drawn from the more than five thousand objects in the personal collection of deceased Standard Oil heiress Millicent Rogers, including strong holdings of Pueblo pottery (among them examples by famed San Ildefonso potter Maria Martinez), Indian silver jewelry and weavings, as well as Hispanic religious and secular arts and crafts. There is also a good gift shop and bookstore.

Details: Take U.S. 64 north from Taos. Just before U.S. 64 turn west (left) onto Millicent Rogers Road and continue several miles south. Open year round, daily 10 A.M.–5 P.M. Closed winter Mondays. Admission is $6 for adults, $5 for seniors and students, and $1 for children. (505) 758-2462.

MUSEUM OF INDIAN ARTS AND CULTURE

This is an attractive, modern institution dedicated to the region's Native arts, including beautiful pottery vessels, stunning silver and turquoise jewelry, fine textiles, and other works created by the state's Pueblo, Apache, and Navajo artists. Galleries display excellent short-term shows on contemporary Indian arts. There is also a good gift shop.

Details: Located in Santa Fe, off Old Santa Fe Trail at 708 Camino Lejo. Open Tue.–Sun. 10 A.M.–5 P.M. Admission is $5 for adults, $1 for New Mexico residents on Sunday (bring a driver's license) and free to New Mexico seniors on Wednesday. Children seventeen and under free. Four-day state museum pass is good here. (505) 827-6344 or www.museumofnewmexico.org

OLD TOWN PLAZA

Here is where Albuquerque got its start as a small village founded by Hispanic farmers in 1706. Around the charming, shady plaza—much calmer and prettier than the highly touted central plazas of Santa Fe and Taos—and down side streets perfect for strolling are hundreds of one-of-a-kind retail stores, art galleries (many of which feature Pueblo artisans), crafts shops, and a handful of restaurants. Bargain directly with the Pueblo arts and crafts vendors who display their excellent goods on blankets under the portal on the east side of the plaza. The Old Town Visitors Center offers tips on the area's attractions and distributes a free walking-tour guide.

Details: Visitors Center at 305 Romero St. NW, Albuquerque. Open Mon.–Sat. 9 A.M.–5 P.M., Sun. 10 A.M.–5 P.M.

PALACE OF THE GOVERNORS

This humble-looking one-story building on the north side of the plaza in Santa Fe has seen an incredible number of important events unfold within its thick adobe walls. The oldest government building in the United States, erected about 1608, it has flown the flags of the Spain, the Republic of Mexico, the United States of America, the Confederate States of America (for a few weeks), and the Territorial flag prior to statehood in 1912. It was also occupied from 1680 to 1692 by an alliance of Pueblo people following the Pueblo Revolt.

Now the state history museum, it provides a great introduction to the region's past. On the building's portal facing the plaza, Pueblo artisans gather daily to display and sell their handmade jewelry, pottery, and other goods. Strict oversight ensures authenticity, so it's a reliable place to shop, and the money goes directly to the artists and craftspeople. The palace also houses a great gift shop and a notable bookstore with locally relevant titles.

Details: Located in Santa Fe on Palace Avenue between Washington and Lincoln Streets. Open Tue.–Sun. 10 A.M.–5 P.M., Fri. to 8 P.M. Admission is $5 for adults. Children under seventeen are free. $1 for New Mexico residents on Sunday (bring a driver's license); free to New Mexico seniors on Wednesday; free to all Friday 5 P.M.–8 P.M. Four-day state museum pass is good here. (505) 827-6483 or www.museumofnewmexico.org

WHEELWRIGHT MUSEUM OF THE AMERICAN INDIAN

Mary Cabot Wheelwright, the Eastern-reared contemporary of more famous Taos arts patron Mabel Dodge Lujan, opened this wonderful, relatively small museum in 1937 to house the work of her close friend Hosteen Klah, a Navajo medicine man, weaver, and sandpainter. Its collections have continued to expand, and today it mounts impressive shows of contemporary and historic art by Native Americans, including Pueblo artists. Its Case Trading Post is a great source for excellent Indian arts and crafts, books, and music.

Details: Located in Santa Fe off Old Santa Fe Trail at 704 Camino Lejo. Open Mon.–Sat. 10 A.M.–5 P.M., Sun. 1–5 P.M. Free. (505) 982-4636.

New Mexico Parks and Monuments

NEW MEXICO HAS A HOST of national and state parks and monuments that have strong associations with ancestral and contemporary Pueblo cultures of the region. Many of these sites preserve and interpret the remains of prehistoric and historic pueblo villages. Visitor center exhibits provide visitors with wonderful windows into the past. Visit these sites to learn more about the origins of today's contemporary Pueblo people.

AZTEC RUINS NATIONAL MONUMENT

This national monument features a reconstructed great kiva—a round, subterranean ceremonial chamber used by the resident Ancestral Pueblo people. Invariably, the roofs of these kivas have not survived the centuries and have collapsed. Archeologist Earl Morris excavated the site in the early twentieth century and rebuilt the cribbed roof using massive pine beams. When you enter this kiva today, it is readily apparent why these spiritual sanctuaries were, and are, so central to Pueblo life.

A 400-yard-long trail winds through the surface ruins, which nineteenth-century Anglo settlers mistakenly believed to be associated with the great Mexican Indian culture. Archeologist Morris debunked this theory. The culture at this site reached its zenith between the twelfth and fourteenth centuries.

Each Christmas Eve, the park service staff and volunteers grace the ruin walls with thousands of farolitos, brown paper bags lit by a votive candle. The visitor center features interactive exhibits and impressive displays of some of the more remarkable objects unearthed at the site. There also is a shady picnic ground.

Details: Located 1.5 miles north of the town of Aztec off NM 550. Open daily Memorial Day through Labor Day, 8 A.M.–6 P.M., otherwise daily 8 A.M.–5 P.M. Admission is $3 for adults. Kids under sixteen are free. (505) 334-6174.

BANDELIER NATIONAL MONUMENT

It's easy to see why Ancestral Pueblo people chose to make their homes in Bandelier National Monument's Frijoles Canyon. The location provided shelter from fierce winter storms that could blanket the surrounding mesas, and the canyon's south-facing cliffs of volcanic tuff were ideal for carving out homes that would be warm in winter and cool in summer. Frijoles Canyon also offered a perennial stream and abundant game. Today, a one-mile asphalt trail winds through a fourteenth-century canyon-floor village, kivas, and cliff dwellings.

Beyond Frijoles Canyon lie 23,000 acres of backcountry wilderness with more than seventy-five miles of hiking and backpacking trails that lead to more isolated ruins and wonderful views. One of the most frequently traveled of these is Falls Trail. The visitor center contains excellent interpretive displays in a small museum setting, and a gift shop.

Details: Located 40 miles west of Santa Fe. Take U.S. 84/285 north to Pojoaque, then exit onto NM 502 and proceed past San Ildefonso Pueblo. Four miles west of the Rio Grande, exit onto NM 4, and then watch for the entrance sign, which will appear on your left. Prior to reaching the main monument, you will pass an outlying site, Tsankawi, which offers a beautiful half-hour hike to unexcavated ruins. Pets are not allowed on national park unit trails. Bandelier's Visitor Center is open daily Memorial Day–Labor Day 8 A.M.–6 P.M., and 9 A.M.–5:30 P.M. while daylight savings is in effect. Hours are 8 A.M.–4:30 P.M. other periods. The park itself is open from dawn to dusk throughout the year. Admission is $10 per vehicle. (505) 672-3861 or (505) 672-0343.

CASAMERO RUINS

Like Aztec Ruins, this small complex of ruins, which features a structure with 22 ground-floor rooms and a small block of second-story rooms, is an outlier of the prehistoric Chaco Canyon culture. The Bureau of Land Management administers the site, which is located just north of I-40 near Thoreau. Call (505) 287-7911 for directions.

CHACO CULTURE NATIONAL HISTORICAL PARK

As all roads once led to Rome, in the prehistoric Southwest they led to Chaco. For several centuries Chaco was the heart of the Ancestral Pueblo world, which stretched from Nevada across north-central Arizona and southern Utah into southwestern

Colorado and northwestern New Mexico. But where Rome tied its empire together through conquest and brute force, the Ancestral Pueblo realm was woven together by delicate threads of trade, spiritual association, and cultural community.

Chaco began to flower around A.D. 900. The Ancestral Pueblo people developed complex social, political, religious, and administrative systems. They built elaborate irrigation systems, multistory stone villages, astronomical observatories, and great kivas. Artists and craftspeople created beautiful pottery, turquoise jewelry, and weavings, while trade goods from the Pacific coast, tropical Mexico, and the Great Plains flowed into the complex. Then in the late twelfth century, the people appear to have dispersed.

Chaco remains off the main tourist track, but visitors can drive up to half of the thirteen principal ruins and hike several short trails that wind through the multistoried pueblos and earthbound kivas. You can also follow backcountry trails to unexcavated sites.

The visitor center displays models, artifacts, audiovisual media, photos, maps, and other interpretive information that explain the significance of Chaco and the role it appears to have played in the Ancestral Pueblo world. You can join tours guided by rangers (May through September) or pick up self-guiding brochures and discover the park's wonders at your own pace.

After orienting yourself at the visitor center, the first major site you will come to along the loop road is Chetro Ketl. This is one of the valley's great houses, with more than five hundred rooms, sixteen kivas, and an enclosed plaza. Nearby is Pueblo Bonito, the largest great house at Chaco and certainly the most famous. Archeologists determined that Pueblo Bonito had been as tall as five stories and had encompassed more than six hundred rooms and forty kivas. At the time of its "discovery" by a U.S. Army detachment in 1849, it was the largest "apartment house" in the United States.

On the south side of the canyon is Casa Rinconada, which harbors Chaco's largest kiva. One can imagine what it must have felt like when it was roofed and one had to crawl through its

entrance tunnel and emerge through a hole in its floor during a ceremony. Flickering firelight would have illuminated singers and drummers amid swirling incense.

Details: To reach Chaco from I-40, exit at Thoreau, which is twenty-nine miles west of Grants and 33 miles east of Gallup, and drive north on NM 371. About five miles north of Crownpoint, turn east (right) onto Navajo Road 9 and proceed 13.5 miles to Seven Lakes. Turn north (left) onto NM 57, a dirt road that runs 20 miles directly into Chaco. From the north, approach on NM 44. Just west of mile marker 112, exit onto the new entrance road, CR 1700. (The old road from Nageezi is now closed, despite what older maps may indicate.) Head southwest on the new road, the first portion of which is paved. The last 16 miles are washboard dirt that is graded only occasionally. Both roads are passable for ordinary cars and RVs in good weather, but be sure to start out with a full tank of gas because none is available in or near the park. Chaco is open year round, but the best time to visit is fall. If time permits, be sure to take a walk on at least one of the park's backcountry trails to see outlying ruins and great canyon views. There is a campground but no food or lodging. The visitor center is open 8 A.M.–6 P.M. in summer, 8 A.M.–5 P.M. otherwise. Admission is $4 per vehicle. (505) 786-7014.

CORONADO STATE MONUMENT

This monument preserves prehistoric Kuaua Pueblo, where you can enter a restored, roofed kiva bedecked with rare wall paintings. The site also provides dramatic views of the Rio Grande Valley below and the nearby Sandia Mountains. A nice visitor center displays materials recovered from the site.

Details: Located west of Bernalillo on the west bank of the Rio Grande, just off NM 44. Open daily 8:30 A.M.–5 P.M. Admission for adults is $2 in winter, $4 in summer. Children under seventeen are free. (505) 867-5351.

EL MORRO NATIONAL MONUMENT

For centuries this prominent landmark with a permanent water source along a natural travel corridor has served as a type of rock blackboard for people passing by. Seven centuries ago, Ancestral Pueblo people settled atop this sandstone bluff and began to leave their marks at the base. The first European to leave an inscription was Don Juan de Oñate, who wrote *paso por aqui*—"passed by here"—in 1605. The Spanish called this landmark El Morro, but by 1857, when a U.S. Army contingent using camels as pack animals tromped through, it was also popularly known as Inscription Rock.

Don't try to add your name to the roll. In 1906, El Morro was declared a national monument, and defacing the rock now is a crime. A visitor center provides information on the monument and associated points of interest. A half-mile asphalt loop trail leads to the inscriptions. If you have an extra hour or two, continue on this trail to the top of the 200-foot-high mesa, where you'll find a beautiful landscape dotted with junipers, ponderosa pine, and the thirteenth-century ruin of Atsinna, once an outlying village of Zuni Pueblo. The entire loop trail is about two miles long.

Details: Located along NM 53, forty-three miles southwest of Grants. Open in summer 9 A.M.– 7 P.M., otherwise 9 A.M.–5 P.M. Admission is $4 per vehicle. (505) 783-4226.

PECOS NATIONAL HISTORICAL PARK

This park preserves the remains of Pecos Pueblo, once one of the largest of the New Mexico pueblos. Located at the mouth of Glorieta Pass, a gateway between the Great Plains and the Rio Grande Valley, it was a major trading center centuries prior to the Spanish arrival. Decimated by introduced diseases, occasional battles with the Spanish, and later by raids of Apache, Comanche, and other nomadic tribes, it was finally abandoned in 1838. A self-guided walking tour includes an opportunity to enter a restored kiva and the ruins of a Franciscan mission church. There is a visitor center with videos, books, and a ranger on duty to answer questions.

Details: Located 25 miles east of Santa Fe off I-25 N. From Exit 307, head east into the village of Pecos, then south 2 miles on NM 63 to the short entrance road. Open Memorial Day through Labor Day, 8 A.M.–6 P.M., otherwise 8 A.M.–5 P.M. Admission is $2 per person or $4 per vehicle. (505) 757-6032.

PETROGLYPH NATIONAL MONUMENT

Long before there was an Albuquerque, Indian people left reminders of their occupation here. On the dark basalt rock cliffs and boulders of West Mesa is one of the world's greatest assemblages of petroglyphs. Among the fifteen thousand drawings pecked into the dark surface of boulders and cliffs are a tropical parrot that suggests contact and trade with prehistoric Mexico, spirals believed to represent the cosmos or eternity, and the hunch-backed flute player Kokopelli, symbol of fertility and frivolity. The images span more than three thousand years, including some rare Spanish and Territorial period petroglyphs.

Details: From Albuquerque, take I-40 west over the Rio Grande to NM 448 (Coors Boulevard North), then turn left off Coors onto Unser Boulevard to 6001 NW. Open daily 8 A.M.–5 P.M. Admission is $1 per car weekdays, $2 weekends. (505) 899-0205.

RED ROCK STATE PARK

This park is home to the annual August Intertribal Indian Ceremonial. It also has a museum of local Indian arts and crafts, and prehistoric Indian artifacts, plus a gift shop and trading post. Located at the foot of a red rock mesa eroded into wonderful spires and domes, it offers short trails that wind back into these formations.

Details: Head east out of Gallup 6 miles on I-40 or Route 66 and then turn north on NM 566. The museum is open weekdays 8:30 A.M.–4:30 P.M., with extended summer hours. (505) 722-3829.

SALINAS PUEBLO MISSIONS NATIONAL MONUMENT

This park protects the remains of three early Catholic mission churches and the pueblos to which they ministered. Thousands of years before the arrival of the Spanish in 1540, Pueblo people made their homes near a handful of salt lakes and ponds southeast of present-day Albuquerque. They collected and traded salt from these waters and became prosperous as traders between the Rio Grande Valley and the Great Plains.

In the 1600s, Spanish priests established mission churches in several of these pueblos, but Apache and other nomadic tribes found the isolated pueblos easy pickings, and the combined effects of repeated raids, epidemics, and droughts led to their abandonment by 1670.

Today the most visible remnants of these communities are the massive stone mission churches the Pueblo people constructed at Abo, Gran Quivira, and Quarai, but the outlines of the pueblos also have been excavated.

Details: A visitor center in Mountainair provides an overview of each site. Each ruin also has its own self-guiding trails and interpretive materials. Abo is located 9 miles west of Mountainair, just off US 60 on NM 513. Quarai is 9 miles north of Mountainair, off NM 55. Gran Quivira, the largest of the ruins, is 26 miles southeast of Mountainair on NM 55. Picnicking is permitted, but not camping. The visitor center and sites are open daily 9 A.M.–5 P.M. and 9 A.M.–6 P.M. in summer. Free. (505) 847-2585.

SALMON RUINS

This privately owned archeological site preserves a relatively small Ancestral Pueblo settlement on the bank of the San Juan River, birthplace of the Ancestral Pueblo culture. It includes a museum and the San Juan Archeological Research Center and Library.

Details: The ruins are located 2 miles west of Bloomfield, just off US 64. Open daily. Admission is $1 for adults, 50 cents for kids. (505) 632-2013.

Suggested Reading

Bahti, Mark. *Pueblo Stories and Storytellers*. Tucson: Treasure Chest Books/Rio Nuevo Publishers, revised edition 1996.

Bahti, Mark. *Southwest Indian Designs*. Tucson: Treasure Chest Books/Rio Nuevo Publishers, revised edition 2001.

Bahti, Mark. *Spirit In the Stone*. Tucson: Treasure Chest Books/Rio Nuevo Publishers, 1999.

Bodine, John J. *Taos Pueblo: A Walk Through Time*. Tucson: Treasure Chest Books/Rio Nuevo Publishers, revised edition 1996.

Branson, Oscar T. *Indian Jewelry Making*. Tucson: Treasure Chest Books/Rio Nuevo Publishers, combined edition 2000.

McManis, Kent. *A Guide to Zuni Fetishes & Carvings, Vol. I: The Animals and the Carvers*. Tucson: Treasure Chest Books/Rio Nuevo Publishers, revised edition 1998.

_____. *A Guide to Zuni Fetishes & Carvings, Vol. II: The Materials and the Carvers*. Tucson: Treasure Chest Books/Rio Nuevo Publishers, 1998.

Acknowledgements

I WOULD LIKE TO THANK THE FOLLOWING individuals who helped make this book a reality.

At the pueblos: Acoma–Brian Vallo, Historic Preservation Office director; Cochiti–Governor Regis Pecos; Jemez–Anita Cajero and Mary Towa, former manager Walatowa Visitor Center; Laguna–Victor Sarracino, chief of operations; Nambe–John Perez, Governor's secretary; Picuris–David Richardson, program manager; Pojoaque–George Rivera, Lt. Governor, and Carol Guzman, administrative assistant; Sandia–Stephine Poston, director Public Relations; San Juan–Herman Agoyo, administrator; Santa Ana–Ben Robbins, administrator; Santa Clara–Nora Baca; Taos–Kathleen Michaels, tourism director; Tesuque–Virgie BigBee, Community Relations director; Zia–Peter Pino, tribal administrator; Zuni–Tom Kennedy, director A:shiwi A:wan Museum and Heritage Center.

The staff of the Museum of New Mexico's photo archive division, particularly Arthur Olivas.

My editor at Rio Nuevo Publishers, Ronald J. Foreman.

Experts in Pueblo arts and crafts, including Rob Lucas, director, Case Trading Post of the Wheelwright Museum, Santa Fe; Dr. Duane Anderson, director, Museum of Indian Arts and Culture, Santa Fe; Don Davies, Packard's, Inc., Santa Fe.

Stanley Pino and family of Zia Pueblo, for their hospitality over the years and many a fine meal. And the people of the pueblos who permit visitors like me to walk through their villages, observe their age-old rituals, and experience their gracious hospitality and fine sense of humor.

My children, Travis and Isabel, who once again put up with a project-obsessed dad.

Photo Credits

Deb Friedrichs:
  47, 49

Mark Nohl:
  back cover inset, 6, 11, 12, 13, 19, 24, 37, 62, 91, 94, 96-97

Stephen Trimble:
  front cover, 2-3, 5, 8, 18, 23, 27, 30, 35, 38, 44, 57, 61, 64, 71, 78-79, 80, 84-85, 89, 90

All archival images courtesy Museum of New Mexico

Edward S. Curtis:
  copyright and table of contents pages (143730), 4 (132696), 67 (144725), 73 (31940)

Mary E. Dissette:
  54 (45441)

Ferenz Fedor:
  41 (100483)

John K. Hillers:
  51 (3371)

William Henry Jackson:
  1 (41729)

Sumner W. Matteson:
  29 (41732)

Jesse L. Nussbaum:
  92 (43170)

T. Harmon Parkhurst:
  half title page (3889), 15 (2647), 16-17 (4011), 25 (55189), 33 (42074), 58-59 (3774), 63 (3860), 75 (2812)

Ben Wittick:
  title pages (16051), 20-21 (16042)

Photographers unknown:
  6-7 (4487), 87 (90901)